Great Misadventures

6/02

Great Misadventures
Bad Ideas That Led to Big Disasters

PEGGY SAARI
EDITED BY BETZ DES CHENES

VOLUME TWO: SCIENCE AND TECHNOLOGY

AN IMPRINT OF GALE

Detroit • London

REF
904
SAA

Great Misadventures:
Bad Ideas That Led to Big Disasters

Peggy Saari

Staff

Elizabeth Des Chenes, *U·X·L Senior Editor*
Carol DeKane Nagel, *U·X·L Managing Editor*
Thomas L. Romig, *U·X·L Publisher*

Margaret Chamberlain, *Permissions Specialist (Pictures)*

Mary Beth Trimper, *Production Director*
Evi Seoud, *Assistant Production Manager*
Deborah Milliken, *Production Assistant*

Cynthia Baldwin, *Product Design Manager*
Michelle Dimercurio, *Art Director*
Linda Mahoney, *Typesetting*

Library of Congress Cataloging-in-Publication Data

Great Misadventures: Bad Ideas That Led to Big Disasters/ Peggy Saari, editor
   v. cm.
     Includes bibliographical references.
     Summary: Explores 100 historical, political, military, and social events
where human error has led to disaster.
     ISBN 0-7876-2798-4 (set: alk. paper). — ISBN 0-7876-2799-2 (v. 1: alk.
paper) — ISBN 0-7876-2800-X (v. 2: alk. paper) — ISBN 0-7876-2801-8 (v. 3:
alk paper) — ISBN 0-7876-2802-6 (v. 4: alk. paper)
     1. History—Miscellanea—Juvenile literature. 2. Disasters—Juvenile litera-
ture. [1. Disasters. 2. History—Miscellanea]
     I. Saari, Peggy.
     D24 G64 1998
     904—dc21
                                   98-13811
                                   CIP

This publication is a creative work fully protected by all applicable copyright laws, as well as by misappropriation, trade secret, unfair competition, and other applicable laws. The editors of this work have added value to the underlying factual material herein through one or more of the following: unique and original selection, coordination, expression, arrangement, and classification of the information. All rights to this publication will be vigorously defended.

Copyright © 1999
U·X·L, an imprint of Gale

All rights reserved, including the right of reproduction in whole or in part in any form.

♾™ This book is printed on acid-free paper that meets the minimum requirements of American National Standard for information Sciences—Permanent Paper for Printed Library Materials, ANSI Z39.48-1984.

Printed in the United States of America

10 9 8 7 6 5 4 3 2

Contents

Reader's Guide xix
Timeline xxi

VOLUME ONE: EXPLORATION AND ADVENTURE

Erik the Red and Norse Settlement
in Greenland **(986 to c. 1500)** 1

> *After a promising start, the Norse settlement in Greenland
> failed due to changing climate conditions.*

The Children's Crusade **(1212)** 7

> *Stephen of Cloyes led an ill-fated children's march to the
> Holy Land that resulted in slavery or death for most of the
> participants.*

Christopher Columbus in
Hispaniola **(1498)** 14

> *The famous explorer ruined his career and reputation by mis-
> managing this early European settlement in the Americas.*

Pedro de Alvarado's Trek
to Quito **(1532 to 1534)** 24

> *After a long and dangerous trip through the Andes
> Mountains, Alvarado discovered that another conquistador
> had already claimed the Incan city of Quito for Spain.*

Francisco de Coronado's Quest
for Gold **(1538 to 1541)** 33

> *While serving as governor of New Galicia, Coronado was
> fooled into launching a futile search for the fabled riches of
> Cibola.*

The Many Misadventures of Sir
Walter Raleigh **(1578 to 1618)** 40

> *A headstrong soldier and adventurer, Raleigh was tried and*
> *executed for disobeying a royal decree.*

The "Lost Colony" at Roanoke
(1588 to 1591) 47

> *The fate of the Roanoke colony—the earliest English settle-*
> *ment in the New World—is one of the biggest mysteries in*
> *American history.*

Willem Barents's Search for a
Northeast Passage **(1596 to 1597)** 53

> *Barents's third attempt to find a northeast passage to Asia*
> *ended in tragedy when his ship became stuck in Arctic ice.*

The Downfall of Rene-Robert
de La Salle **(1687)** 58

> *After experiencing a series of disastrous setbacks while*
> *exploring the area around the Gulf of Mexico, La Salle was*
> *attacked and killed by his own men.*

James Cook in the South Pacific
and Antarctica **(1768 to 1780)** 65

> *Cook's expeditions devastated the lives of native peoples*
> *by introducing disease and unfamiliar customs into their*
> *cultures.*

Mungo Park's Second Trip to the
Niger River **(1806)** 75

> *On his second trip to the Niger River area, Park made sev-*
> *eral crucial miscalculations that resulted in his death.*

Peter Skene Ogden and the
Columbia River Territory **(1824 to 1830)** 83

> *In an ironic twist, Ogden's explorations for the British-held*
> *Hudson's Bay Company were instrumental in determining*
> *the boundaries of what later became United States territory.*

The Donner Party Tragedy
(April 1846 to April 1847) 90

> *Members of the Donner Party resorted to cannibalism after*
> *becoming stranded in the Sierra Nevada mountain range.*

The Disappearance of John Franklin's
Expedition **(1847)** 96

For nearly a decade, the British government tried to discover what had happened to Franklin and his men in the Canadian Arctic.

David Livingstone's African
Expeditions **(June 1849 to October 1873)** 104

Livingstone's adventures in Africa—including his famous search for the source of the Nile River—were often marked by personal tragedy.

Burke and Wills Seek Telegraph
Route **(August 1860 to June 1861)** 114

The Burke-Wills trip, which accomplished nothing of real value, was the costliest government-sponsored expedition in Australian history.

Francis Garnier's Death in Vietnam
(December 21, 1873) 122

Garnier's impulsive actions caused French forces to lose control of the Vietnamese city of Hanoi for over ten years.

George Washington De Long's Search
for the North Pole **(June 1879 to June 1881)** 129

De Long and several of his crewmen died while trying to prove that it was possible to reach the North Pole via the Bering Strait.

Frederick Albert Cook's "Discovery"
of the North Pole **(April 21, 1908)** 135

Later labeled a liar and a fraud, Cook claimed to have reached the North Pole before his main rival, explorer Robert Peary.

Robert Falcon Scott's Trip to the
South Pole **(June 1, 1910 to March 29(?), 1912)** 144

Scott and his crew were plagued by terrible misfortunes during most of their second polar expedition, including a leaky ship, dead sledge ponies, and competition from a Norwegian team led by explorer Roald Amundsen.

Umberto Nobile and the *Italia*
Crash **(May 1928)** 151

Nobile's reputation as an airship designer and commander suffered after the Italia crashed during a flight to the Arctic.

The Disappearance of
Amelia Earhart **(June 1937)** 157

> Earhart's mysterious disappearance over the Pacific Ocean
> has baffled aviation experts for decades.

Christopher McCandless in the
Alaskan Wilderness **(April 1992 to
August 1992)** 164

> As a result of his poor preparation and limited experience,
> McCandless suffered a long and painful death in the back-
> woods of Alaska.

Jessica Dubroff's Fatal Flight
(April 8, 1996 to April 11, 1996) 174

> Seven-year-old Dubroff, along with her father and her flying
> instructor, crashed while trying to set a controversial
> transcontinental flight record.

Fatalities on Mount Everest
(May 10 and 11, 1996) 180

> In the worst single disaster on Everest, seven mountain
> climbers died when they were trapped in a blizzard on the
> summit.

Picture Credits xxxi
Index xxxiii

VOLUME TWO: SCIENCE AND TECHNOLOGY

Copper Mining in Butte,
Montana **(1876 to 1983)** 191

> More than 100 years after its first copper mines opened,
> Butte has become one of the worst environmental disaster
> sites in the United States.

The Sinking of the *Titanic*
(April 14, 1912) 198

> The "practically unsinkable" Titanic sank with over 1,500
> passengers after hitting an iceberg off the coast of
> Newfoundland.

The Boston Molasses Spill
(January 15, 1919) 209

> Twenty-one people were killed and several blocks in Boston's
> North End were destroyed after a poorly constructed holding
> tank exploded.

The Failure of the Artificial Heart
(1935 to 1990) 214

> *After several implantation surgeries failed, the Food and Drug Administration withdrew its approval of the Jarvik-7 artificial heart.*

The *Hindenburg* Airship Crash
(May 6, 1937) 220

> *Explanations for the fiery Hindenburg crash have ranged from sabotage to a stray lightning strike.*

DDT Contamination **(1939 to present)** 230

> *Scientists have determined that the widespread use of DDT has contaminated the entire food chain.*

Love Canal Toxic Waste
Contamination **(beginning in 1942)** 237

> *The term "Love Canal" has become synonymous with toxic waste mismanagement.*

Howard Hughes and the
Spruce Goose **(1942 to 1947)** 244

> *Even after his plane's design and purpose had become obsolete, Hughes continued to work on enhancements to the Spruce Goose seaplane.*

Thalidomide Birth Defects
(late 1950s to early 1960s) 253

> *Within six years of its introduction, Thalidomide—widely marketed as an anti-nausea drug—was found to cause birth defects in thousands of babies.*

TWA Super-Constellation and
United Airlines DC-7 Collision
(June 30, 1956) 259

> *This deadly crash over empty airspace in the Grand Canyon led to an overhaul of the air traffic control system.*

Chevrolet Corvair Controversy
(1959 to 1963) 265

> *After a series of fatal accidents, the Corvair's suspension and heating systems' design came under intense scrutiny.*

Agent Orange Spraying **(1961 to 1971)** 273

> *Veterans claim that heavy spraying of the defoliant Agent Orange during the Vietnam War can be directly linked to cancer and other diseases.*

The *Apollo 13* Oxygen Tank Rupture 282
(April 13, 1970)

Even though the Apollo 13 crew was able to overcome the effects of the tank explosion, the accident left many observers questioning the need for repeated manned lunar landings.

Ford Pinto Rear-Impact Defect 289
(1971 to 1976)

The Ford Motor Company recalled 1.4 million Pinto auto-mobiles after several deadly fuel tank accidents.

Three Mile Island Meltdown 295
(March 28, 1979)

A partial meltdown at this Pennsylvania nuclear power plant became a turning point in the public's attitude toward nuclear power.

MGM Grand Hotel Fire 302
(November 21, 1980)

The MGM Grand Hotel fire led to a dramatic increase in the updating of fire code regulations.

The Superconducting Super Collider 309
(early 1980s to 1993)

The U.S. Congress voted to cut funds for the SSC project after six years of construction problems and cost overruns.

Toxic Vapor Leak in Bhopal, India 315
(December 3, 1984)

This deadly gas leak at a Union Carbide plant located in a heavily populated area left thousands of people dead and many more badly injured.

The *Challenger* Explosion **(January 28, 1986)** 320

The failure of the shuttle's solid rocket O-rings triggered an explosion that killed everyone on board.

Chernobyl Accident in the Ukraine 331
(April 26, 1986)

Considered the world's worst nuclear disaster, the Chernobyl accident occurred after the plant crew decided to carry out a controlled experiment.

Exxon *Valdez* Oil Spill **(March 24, 1989)** 338

More then 1,500 miles of Alaska shoreline were polluted after the Valdez ran aground on Bligh Reef.

The "Year 2000" Computer Problem
(1990s) 345

An early software and hardware programming decision created a huge crisis for computer users around the world.

The Ban on Silicone Breast Implants
(1992) 351

After years of controversy surrounding their safety, silicone breast implants were banned by the U.S. Food and Drug Administration.

Mad Cow Disease Outbreak (1996) 357

The British government caused an international crisis when it announced that ten people had died after eating meat from cattle infected with BSE, or mad cow disease.

The Death of Dr. Karen Wetterhan
(1997) 365

The death of a university scientist sparked a national debate about the safety of laboratories involved in chemical research.

Picture Credits xxxi
Index xxxiii

VOLUME THREE: MILITARY

The Fall of Athens (415 B.C. to 413 B.C.) 371

Athenian leaders never suspected that one of their own fleet commanders would betray them in battle.

Alexander in the Gedrosia Desert
(325 B.C) 377

Nearly 60,000 people—including many women and children—died during Alexander the Great's ill-advised journey through the Gedrosia Desert.

The Battle of Hattin (1187) 386

Crusader forces lost control of Jerusalem after falling into a trap set by the Muslim leader Saladin.

The English Expedition to Cádiz
(1625) 393

The British expedition to Cádiz, Spain, demonstrated how far the English navy's readiness had deteriorated.

The Battle of Poltava (1709) 400

The Swedish army suffered a crushing defeat at the hands of the Russians when two of its generals could not stop squabbling with each other.

The Battle of Trenton
(December 26, 1776) 405

American general George Washington won a decisive Revolutionary War victory when the enemy commander underestimated the rebel army's strength.

Tecumseh's Campaign
(mid-1790s to 1813) 409

Tecumseh, a Shawnee war chief, led an ultimately unsuccessful crusade to create an Indian confederacy.

The Fall of Detroit (August 16, 1812) 417

After firing only one shot, British forces were able to retake Fort Detroit and achieve an important victory in the War of 1812.

The Battle of Waterloo (June 18, 1815) 425

Troops under the command of French emperor Napoléon Bonaparte met defeat after their leader made a tactical blunder.

The Crimean War
(October 1853 to February 1856) 433

Thousands of British soldiers became severely ill or died when their supply units failed to distribute medicine, warm clothes, and fresh food.

Francisco Solano Lopez Destroys
Paraguay (1862 to 1870) 440

Paraguayan dictator Lopez devastated his country in a doomed attempt to win the "War of the Triple Alliance."

The Assault on Fort Wagner
(July 1863) 445

Union troops—including the elite African American 54th Massachusetts Regiment—suffered heavy losses during their attack on this Confederate stronghold.

Pickett's Charge (July 1863) 454

Flawed military strategy and lack of communication caused Confederate soldiers to march to their deaths during this skirmish at the Battle of Gettysburg.

The Battle of Little Bighorn
(June 25, 1876) 463

Lieutenant Colonel George Armstrong Custer and the entire 7th Cavalry were killed in this battle between government troops and thousands of Sioux and Cheyenne warriors.

Gallipoli Campaign
(February 1915 to January 1916) 469

Considered one of the most disastrous battles of World War I, the Allies' Gallipoli campaign was marked by disorganization and poor leadership.

The Battle of Verdun
(February 1916 to October 1916) 476

Much to the German army's surprise, the French forces at Verdun refused to give up their ancient city without a strong and very bloody fight.

The Easter Rising
(April 24, 1916, to April 26, 1916) 487

Organizers of the Easter Rising in Dublin, Ireland, knew that their rebellion against British rule was doomed from the start.

The Amritsar Massacre **(April 13, 1919)** 496

The killing of over 370 unarmed protestors by British troops in Amritsar, India, created widespread support for the Indian independence movement.

Operation Barbarossa **(1941 to 1942)** 502

German leader Adolf Hitler's invasion of Russia ended in retreat due to a poor battle strategy and incompetent leadership.

Kamikaze at Leyte Gulf
(October 21 to October 26, 1944) 512

Using an ill-conceived "all or nothing" battle plan, the elite Japanese kamikaze fleet was nearly destroyed by Allied forces in the Philippines.

Douglas MacArthur in Korea
(1950 to 1951) 521

MacArthur's illustrious military career came to an end when he was charged with insubordination by President Harry S Truman.

The Bay of Pigs Invasion **(April 17, 1961)** 529
> *This CIA-backed military plot to overthrow Cuban president Fidel Castro failed when the Cuban exiles executing the plan were overwhelmed by Castro's troops.*

The Vietnam War **(1961 to 1973)** 536
> *Spanning the administrations of four American presidents, the war in Vietnam proved to be a catastrophe for U.S. government and military leaders.*

Operation Eagle Claw
(April 24 to April 25, 1980) 546
> *American president Jimmy Carter approved this unsuccessful mission to save Americans held hostage in Iran by followers of the Ayatollah Khomeini.*

The Persian Gulf War
(January to February 1991) 553
> *This 100-hour conflict—declared a victory by the American-led coalition forces—failed to remove Iraqi leader Saddam Hussein from power.*

Picture Credits xxxi
Index xxxiii

VOLUME FOUR: SOCIETY

Cleopatra's Fall **(30 B.C.)** 561
> *In an attempt to regain Egypt's lost political status, Cleopatra formed complicated, and ultimately futile, alliances with two Roman leaders.*

The Romance of Heloise and
Abelard **(1118)** 567
> *The letters written between these ill-fated twelfth-century lovers about philosophical and political issues have become legendary.*

Witchcraft Hysteria **(1486 to c. 1700)** 575
> *The publication of the* Malleus Maleficarum, *an encyclopedia of contemporary knowledge about witchcraft, set the stage for over 200 years of religious persecution.*

The Gunpowder Plot **(November 5, 1605)** 580

> *In an attempt to overthrow the Protestant monarchy, a group of English Roman Catholics devised this scheme to blow up the British Parliament and kill King James I.*

The Luddite Movement **(1811 to 1816)** 585

> *Faced with losing their livelihoods to mechanization, the Luddites destroyed factory machinery in an effort to slow technological progress.*

The Southampton Insurrection
(August 21 to 24, 1831) 591

> *Nat Turner, a black slave and preacher, led this short-lived and violent revolt against Southern slaveholders.*

John Brown's Raid **(October 16 to 18, 1859)** 595

> *Brown's failed raid on the federal armory at Harpers Ferry— an attempt to gain arms for a war against slavery—only served to increase tensions between the North and the South.*

The Triangle Shirtwaist
Company Fire **(March 25, 1911)** 600

> *The Triangle fire was one of the worst industrial disasters in American history, resulting in the deaths of 146 company employees.*

The Black Sox Baseball Scandal **(1919)** 607

> *Eight members of the Chicago White Sox baseball team were banned from playing the game for life after participating in a conspiracy to fix the World Series.*

The Dionne Quintuplets **(born in 1934)** 615

> *Soon after their birth, the identical Dionne quintuplets became wards of the state and were put on public display.*

The *War of the Worlds* Broadcast
(October 31, 1938) 621

> *This famous* Mercury Theatre on the Air *presentation about a fictional Martian invasion created widespread panic when millions of radio listeners thought that the attack was real.*

The McCarthy Communist Scare
(1950 to 1954) 626

> *Wisconsin senator Joseph R. McCarthy gained fame and political power after he claimed that Communists had infiltrated several levels of American government.*

The Rosenberg Case
(June 15, 1950 to June 19, 1950) 633

After a controversial trial that attracted international atten-
tion, Julius and Ethel Rosenberg became the first U.S. citi-
zens to be executed for espionage.

The *Twenty-One* Quiz Show Scandal
(1956 to 1959) 641

Academic Charles Van Doren became an overnight celebrity
after he agreed to participate in a quiz show answer-fixing
scheme.

The Watergate Cover-Up **(1972 to 1974)** 650

The arrest of five men for a burglary at the offices of the
Democratic National Committee erupted into a scandal that
led to the resignation of President Richard M. Nixon.

Big-Budget Movie Mania **(1977 to present)** 660

The drive for higher profits at any cost led many movie stu-
dios to approve risky projects with huge budgets, often with
disastrous results.

Denver International Airport
Construction **(1984 to 1994)** 669

Plagued by construction delays, mechanical problems, and
charges of financial impropriety on the part of contractors and
public officials, the DIA nearly failed to open for business.

The Aldrich Ames Spy Case
(1985 to 1994) 675

Ames, a troubled CIA operative, committed the most dam-
aging act of betrayal in the agency's history.

The Fall of John Gotti **(1990 to 1992)** 684

After an intensive FBI investigation, powerful Mafia boss
Gotti, along with many of his henchmen, was arrested and
put on trial.

The Sinking of the *Andrea Gail* **(October 28, 1991)** 691

The loss of this fishing boat during the "storm of the centu-
ry" reflected the inherent dangers of commercial fishing, a
profession that has not essentially changed in over 300
years.

The Assault on Nancy Kerrigan
(January 6, 1994) 696

Ice skater Tonya Harding saw her dreams of fame and fortune die after she became the prime suspect in an attack on her foremost skating rival.

Nicholas Leeson and the Collapse of
Barings PLC **(1995)** 703

Trader Leeson rocked the financial industry when he triggered the collapse of one of the oldest and most trusted banking institutions in the world.

The Tokyo Nerve Gas Strike
(March 20, 1995) 711

In the aftermath of a terrorist attack on the Japanese subway system, an obscure religious sect and its mysterious leader became the primary focus of the government's investigation.

Hostage Crisis in Peru
(December 17, 1996 to April 13, 1997) 717

Peruvian president Alberto Fujimori made headlines around the world when he refused to deal with terrorists holding Japanese embassy staff members hostage.

The Bre-X Mining Scandal **(1997)** 724

In a wide-ranging scandal involving gold, fraudulent stocks, and a mysterious death, officials of the Bre-X Mining company were accused of cheating hundreds of investors out of millions of dollars.

Picture Credits xxxi
Index xxxiii

Reader's Guide

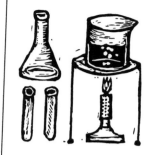

Great *Misadventures: Bad Ideas That Led to Big Disasters* presents 100 stories of human error, greed, and poor judgment that span history from ancient times through the present. Each entry, whether on an infamous adventure, a technological failure, a deadly battle, or a social calamity, offers historical background and a vivid description of the event, together with a discussion about why the misadventure is significant.

In many cases, a misadventure had a positive outcome—laws were enacted, failure led to progress, the protagonist became a national hero—but in others, death or destruction were the only result. It is disillusioning to learn, for example, that a great explorer committed atrocities, or that a well-known celebrity was a liar. It is equally disturbing to discover that incompetent leaders caused needless loss of life in wars, or that cutting-edge technology was sometimes useless or even dangerous. The goal of *Great Misadventures* is to show that success can also involve failure, triumph can encompass defeat, and human beings are inspired by self-interest as often as they are motivated by selflessness.

Format

The *Great Misadventures* entries are arranged chronologically within four subject volumes: Exploration and Adventure, Science and Technology, Military, and Society. Cross references direct users to related entries throughout the four-volume set, while sources for further reference at the end of each entry offer more information on featured people and events. Call-out boxes present biographical profiles and fascinating facts, and more than 220 black-and-white photographs, illustrations, and

maps help illuminate the text. Each volume contains an anno-
tated table of contents, a timeline of important events, and a
cumulative index.

Comments and Suggestions

We welcome your comments and suggestions for subjects
to feature in future editions of *Great Misadventures*. Please
write: Editors, *Great Misadventures*, U•X•L, 27500 Drake Rd.,
Farmington Hills, Michigan, 48331–3535; call toll-free:
800–877–4253; or fax 1–800–414–5043.

Timeline

415 B.C. Athenian naval commander Alcibiades is defeated during an assault on Syracuse.

325 B.C. Macedonian leader Alexander the Great leads a tragic expedition across the Gedrosia desert.

30 B.C. Egyptian queen Cleopatra commits suicide.

1118 French philosopher Peter Abelard begins a tragic love affair with his student Héloise.

1187 Christian Crusaders lose the Battle of Hattin to the Muslims.

1212 Stephen of Cloyes, a French shepherd boy, leads the ill-fated Children's Crusade.

1498 Italian explorer Christopher Columbus begins his rule of Hispaniola.

c. 1500 The Norse settlement in Greenland is abandoned.

1533 Spanish conquistador Pedro de Alvarado leads a disastrous trek across the Andes.

1541 Spanish conquistador Francisco Vázquez de Coronado fails to find the Seven Cities of Cibola.

214 B.C
Great Wall of
China is built

1215
Magna Carta
is written

1455
War of the Roses
begins

250 B.C.   1100   1300   1500

1591 English colonists disappear from the Roanoke settlement.

1597 Dutch explorer Willem Barents dies in a failed attempt to find a northeast sea passage to Asia.

1605 English Roman Catholics fail to blow up Parliament as part of the Gunpowder Plot.

1618 English explorer Sir Walter Raleigh is beheaded for disobeying King James I.

1625 The British fleet is defeated in a disastrous misadventure at the port of Cádiz, Spain.

1687 French explorer René-Robert de La Salle is killed by his own men.

1709 The Swedish army loses the Battle of Poltava because of a squabble between two of its commanders.

1776 Hessian colonel Johann Gottlieb Rall loses the Battle of Trenton when he underestimates rebel troop strength.

1779 English explorer James Cook is murdered by angry Hawaiian islanders.

1806 Scottish explorer Mungo Park drowns during an expedition on the Niger River.

1811 Rebellious English textile workers calling themselves "Luddites" begin a failed uprising against the Industrial Revolution.

1812 Poor leadership by American general William Hull leads to the Fall of Detroit during the War of 1812.

1815 French leader Napoléon Bonaparte is defeated by British forces at the Battle of Waterloo.

1831 African American slave Nat Turner leads the failed Southampton Insurrection.

1618
Thirty Years'
War begins

1770
The
Enlightenment
ends

1805
Lewis and Clark
reach the
Pacific Ocean

1600   1700   1800

1844 Canadian trapper Peter Skene Ogden explores territory for Britain that is later lost to the United States in a land dispute.

1846 Donner Party members resort to cannibalism after being trapped in the Sierra Nevada.

1847 British explorer John Franklin is lost at sea during his search for the Northwest Passage.

1855 Deprivations during the Crimean War lead to an overwhelming number of deaths among British soldiers.

1859 Abolitionist John Brown stages a failed raid on the federal arsenal at Harpers Ferry, Virginia.

1861 Australian explorers Robert O'Hara Burke and William John Wills starve to death during their transcontinental expedition.

1863 Confederate general George Edward Pickett marches his troops to certain death at the Battle of Gettysburg.

1863 The African American 54th Massachusetts Regiment stages an heroic but unsuccessful assault on Fort Wagner, South Carolina.

1870 Paraguay's male population is reduced by almost ninety percent during the "War of the Triple Alliance."

1873 British missionary and explorer David Livingstone dies during his final adventure in Africa.

1873 French explorer Francis Garnier makes a tactical error that ends French control of the Vietnamese city of Hanoi.

1876 The 7th Cavalry is annihilated by Sioux and Cheyenne warriors at the Battle of Little BigHorn.

1881 American explorer George Washington De Long and his crew are lost while attempting to find a route to the North Pole through the Bering Strait.

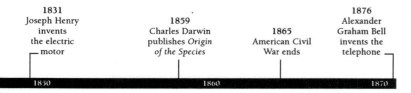

1831
Joseph Henry
invents
the electric
motor

1859
Charles Darwin
publishes *Origin
of the Species*

1865
American Civil
War ends

1876
Alexander
Graham Bell
invents the
telephone

1850   1860   1870

1908 American explorer Frederick Albert Cook claims to be the first man to reach the North Pole.

1911 One hundred and forty-six immigrant workers perish in the Triangle Shirtwaist Company fire in New York City.

1912 British explorer Robert Falcon Scott and his party freeze to death on their return trip from the South Pole.

1912 The luxury ocean liner *Titanic* sinks after hitting an iceberg.

1915 Poor leadership and bad communication leads to high Allied casualties at the Battle of Gallipoli.

1916 Irish revolutionaries stage the unsuccessful Easter Rising.

1919 A steel tank containing 12,000 tons of molasses bursts open in Boston, Massachusetts, and kills twenty-one people.

1919 British troops kill 379 unarmed Indian protestors during the Amritsar Massacre.

1920 Seven Chicago White Sox players are banned from playing baseball for their role in the "Black Sox" betting scandal.

1928 Italian pilot Umberto Nobile crashes the airship *Italia* during a flight to the North Pole.

1934 The Dionne quintuplets are born in Canada and soon become a tourist and media attraction.

1937 American aviator Amelia Earhart and her navigator Fred Noonan are lost on a flight across the Pacific Ocean.

1937 The airship *Hindenberg* explodes after landing in Lakehurst, New Jersey.

1938 The *War of the Worlds* radio broadcast about a fictional Martian invasion causes widespread public panic.

1902 Cuba achieves independence	1914 World War I begins		1929 Great Depression begins
1900	1910	1920	1930

1941 German leader Adolf Hitler launches Operation Barbarossa, his failed invasion of Russia.

1944 The Japanese navy and air force stage a futile kamikaze attack at the Battle of Leyte Gulf.

1947 American inventor Howard Hughes flies his *Spruce Goose* seaplane for ninety seconds.

1950 U.S. senator Joseph McCarthy launches his four-year search for Communist infiltrators.

1951 U.S. general Douglas MacArthur is relieved of his command during the Korean War.

1953 Julius and Ethel Rosenberg become the first U.S. citizens to be executed for espionage.

1956 A United Airlines DC-7 and a TWA Constellation collide in empty air space over the Grand Canyon.

1956 American college instructor Charles Van Doren becomes involved in the *Twenty-One* quiz show scandal.

1961 CIA-trained Cuban refugees fail to overthrow dictator Fidel Castro during the Bay of Pigs invasion.

1961 The U.S. Air Force begins spraying the defoliant Agent Orange in Vietnam.

1969 General Motors discontinues production of the controversial Chevrolet Corvair, America's first rear-engine automobile.

1970 American astronauts abort the *Apollo 13* mission to the Moon.

1972 A failed burglary at the offices of the Democratic National Committee sets the stage for the Watergate scandal.

1973 The United States ends its long and disastrous military involvement in the Vietnam War.

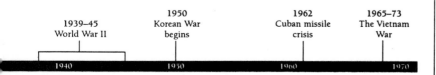

1939–45 World War II	1950 Korean War begins	1962 Cuban missile crisis	1965–73 The Vietnam War
1940	1950	1960	1970

1978 The Ford Motor Company recalls 1.4 million Pinto automobiles after several fatal rear-impact collisions.

1979 The Three Mile Island nuclear power plant in Pennsylvania has an accidental meltdown.

1980 Love Canal, New York, is evacuated after years of toxic waste dumping make this residential area uninhabitable.

1980 Fire protection systems fail to prevent a blaze from engulfing the MGM Grand Hotel in Las Vegas, Nevada.

1980 U.S. military forces stage an aborted rescue of American hostages in Tehran, Iran.

1983 Artificial heart recipient Barney Clark dies 112 days after his historic surgery.

1983 The infamous copper mining "Pit" in Butte, Montana is closed.

1984 A poisonous gas cloud escapes from the Union Carbide chemical plant in Bhopal, India, killing thousands of people.

1986 Two mammoth explosions blow apart Unit 4 of the Chernobyl nuclear power plant in the Ukraine.

1986 The entire flight crew dies when the space shuttle *Challenger* explodes after launch.

1989 The oil tanker Exxon *Valdez* runs aground in Alaska, spilling 10.8 million gallons of crude oil and polluting 1,500 miles of shoreline.

1991 U.S. diplomatic failures help trigger the Persian Gulf War.

1992 Silicone breast implants are banned by the Food and Drug Administration.

1992 John Gotti, the "Teflon Don," is sentenced to life in prison after his underboss, Sammy "the Bull" Gravano, testifies against the Gambino crime family.

1974
President Richard M.
Nixon resigns

1983
The United States
invades Grenada

1989
The Berlin
Wall is
destroyed

1975   1980   1985

1992 American adventurer Christopher McCandless starves to death during an Alaskan wilderness trek.

1993 The U.S. Congress ends funding for the Superconductor Super Collider.

1994 U.S. figure skater Tanya Harding is implicated in an assault on fellow skater Nancy Kerrigan.

1994 CIA agent Aldrich Ames is convicted of spying for the Soviet Union.

1995 Twelve people die and thousands are injured in a nerve gas attack in Tokyo, Japan.

1995 English stock trader Nicholas Leeson triggers the collapse of Barings PLC.

1995 The controversial Denver International Airport in Colorado finally opens for business.

1996 The British government orders the slaughter of thousands of cattle infected with mad cow disease.

1996 Seven-year-old American pilot Jessica Dubroff dies while trying to set an aviation record.

1996 Seven climbers perish during a blizzard on Mount Everest.

1997 The MRTA hostage crisis at the Japanese embassy in Lima, Peru, reaches a violent climax.

1997 The Canadian Bre-X mining company is shut down after the world's largest "gold discovery" proves to be a hoax.

1997 American scientist Karen Wetterhahn dies after being exposed to liquid mercury during a laboratory experiment.

1998 Federal Aviation Administration technicians conclude that the mainframe computer used in the nation's largest air traffic control centers is "Year 2000" compliant.

Great Misadventures

Copper Mining in Butte, Montana

1876 TO 1983

T he infamous "Pit" that dominates the middle of the once great copper-mining city of Butte, Montana, was finally closed in 1983. The great hole is a reminder of a once-successful enterprise that ended in disaster. The Pit's story began in 1876 when copper was discovered in the Montana town. Four years later, a huge corporation, the Anaconda Copper Mining Company, moved into Butte. By 1927 Anaconda owned almost all of the mines in the area. As time and mining development went on, workers became angry about unsafe mining conditions. Even after the 1917 Speculator Mine fire—the worst hardrock mining disaster in American history—the Anaconda Company would not ease its merciless grip. Copper mining was big business, and even strikes and uprisings set in motion by the International Workers of the World (IWW) did not slow down its growth. More than 100 years after its first copper mines opened, however, Butte has become the site of one of the worst environmental disasters in America.

Butte once stood as a shining example of progress in the vast desert of the American West.

A center for mining activity

Long before Butte became one of America's worst environmental sites, the city was a boomtown. The discovery of copper in the Butte area in 1876 coincided with the production of

191

THE WORST HARDROCK MINING DISASTER

Any type of mining, whether for gold, iron, or coal, is hard and dangerous work. Copper mining in Butte, Montana, offered an example of what could happen as the result of unsafe labor conditions. From 1900 until 1925, one miner died in an accident every other day in Butte. Miners had to endure a variety of health hazards, including silicosis (a lung condition caused by inhalation of rock dust) and even the plague (a highly contagious disease). Many of the miners also caught pneumonia (a disease of the lungs) after emerging from 100-degree mining tunnels into the freezing Montana winters. The difference in temperature was often so great that men literally exploded in a cloud of steam after surfacing from a mine. Unfortunately, work-related illness and death were features of everyday life in Butte.

The greatest danger confronted by workers was a mine shaft fire. The worst mine shaft fire in Butte was the Speculator Mine fire that occurred on the evening of June 8, 1917. Miners had been working day and night to supply copper for the U.S. Army, which had just entered World War I. Overwork was blamed as the cause of the terrible fire. At 11:45 P.M., the shift boss descended into the main tunnel to untangle an electrical cable. When his lantern touched the frayed insulation (protective covering) of a wire that was saturated with oil, the entire 3,000-foot-long mine shaft caught fire. The fire and caustic smoke claimed 169 lives. Despite the dangers, however, copper mining in Butte thrived until the demand for copper came to a crashing halt later in the century.

the telephone, which used copper wiring, and the Philadelphia Centennial Exhibition, a showcase for other electrical inventions that required copper wiring. The resulting technological revolution turned the small tent village housing 300 men into a city where more than $1 million worth of copper ore was produced every month. Butte quickly expanded into a major western city with banks, breweries, cigar factories, and more than 100 saloons. In its heyday, Butte was a bigger commercial center than Houston, Texas, and Phoenix, Arizona. Five different railroads converged in the great city, and thirty passenger trains stopped there daily. Butte also featured America's first electric train.

In the early 1900s, copper wiring was used for electricity in all houses and buildings, and all the copper ore came from Butte. During World War I (1914–18) copper was also used to make ammunition. In fact, every single American bullet fired in the war contained at least one ounce of copper. As a result, in 1917 the copper mining industry was at its highest point, and Butte was the center of the nation's mining activity.

Butte eventually became the largest Superfund site in the United States. Superfund area cleanup targets—like the Bridgeport Rental and Oil Service site in New Jersey (pictured above)—are paid for out of the national budget.

Workers flocked from all over the world to get jobs in the growing city. In 1917, Butte was home to 96,000 people, not including journeymen (traveling laborers). At the time, the Montana city stood as a shining example of progress in the middle of the desert in the American West.

Anaconda forms monopoly

Many of the immigrants arriving at Ellis Island in New York City (America's chief entry station for immigrants from 1892–1943) did not speak English. People who wanted to be transferred to Butte only had to show a photograph of the seven familiar smokestacks of Butte's Neversweat Mine to tell officials where they were going. The Neversweat Mine was one of the sites owned by the Anaconda Copper Mining Company, the fourth largest corporation in the world. Anaconda was founded in 1880 by Marcus Daly (1841–1900). The company's success was fueled by the increasing demand for copper, which eventually turned Anaconda into a corporate giant. By 1927 the Anaconda Company owned almost every mine in Butte.

A labor battleground

The Anaconda monopoly, however, grew at the expense of worker exploitation. Soon Butte became the battleground for one of the worst confrontations between labor and industry in American history. Both sides of the struggle were strong. Against Anaconda stood one of the best-organized labor forces in America. Labor activism began with the Butte Miner's Union, which was formed in 1878 to protect miners from the dangers of working underground. The Butte delegation was the largest at the 1906 founding convention of the IWW in Chicago, Illinois. One of the organizers of the IWW, the famous labor leader Frank Little, became involved in worker strikes in Butte.

Worker uprisings took place in the city streets and in the mines. Angry miners fought company officials with rocks and bottles; sometimes they used guns and dynamite. The first major labor-management confrontation in Butte took place in 1914 and lasted ten days, during which the IWW bombed the Miner's Union hall. The state of Montana responded by calling in the National Guard to restore order, but the workers continued their revolt. Then, on June 8, 1917, the worst hardrock mining disaster in American history—the Speculator Mine fire—caused the deaths of 169 men. (Hardrock mining involves cutting through layers of rock to extract, or remove, ore.) Afterward the fire, workers became angrier than ever, demanding better safety measures. When Anaconda refused, 15,000 men went on strike. This confrontation lasted sixteen months. During this time the National Guard continued to patrol the streets of Butte, and Little was hanged by Anaconda thugs on August 1, 1917.

A bloody climax

Over the next few years, the strikes continued despite state intervention. In 1918 the IWW was outlawed under the Montana Sedition Act, which—among other things—banned free speech. Finally, on April 21, 1920, the battle came to a bloody climax. The IWW was picketing (protesting) illegally

MULTI-ETHNIC POPULATION The copper-mining city of Butte, Montana, was built in the middle of the great American desert. Yet at the end of the nineteenth century it had a multi-ethnic population similar to eastern metropolitan areas such as New York City; Baltimore, Maryland; and Boston, Massachusetts. Chinese, Italian, German, Jewish, Croatian, Serbian, Finnish, and Spanish immigrants flocked to Butte to work in the mines or related businesses. (In fact, many Chinese workers had already been in America building railroads when they moved on to Butte to mine copper.) By 1900 America's fourth-largest immigration office was in Butte, and a 1918 survey reported that Butte families had origins in thirty-eight countries.

on Anaconda Road in front of the Neversweat mine yard. Suddenly, Anaconda guards started shooting at the picketers with machine guns. The guards killed two men and injured thirteen others. This time the state called in the U.S. Army to restore and maintain order. In the end, business continued despite worker complaints.

Butte a ghost town

After several decades of prosperity, the city of Butte succumbed to a decreasing demand for copper. After World War I, there was no longer a great demand for copper. The biggest blow to the copper industry, however, occurred later in the century when copper wiring became antiquated (or outdated). Aluminum replaced copper in electrical wiring for houses and buildings. Then, as technology became more advanced, the advent of fiber optics (thin glass wire) for telephone communication, along with the use of wireless satellite broadcasting (devices that pick up and transmit electronic waves through space), made even aluminum wiring obsolete. Any copper still needed was imported from foreign countries. Butte felt this shift in technology as early as the 1950s. The resulting full-scale migration from the city eventually turned Butte into a ghost town.

The "Pit" dominates city

After most of the mine shafts (deep tunnels through which minerals are carried to the surface) closed in the 1950s, busi-

BUTTE DIVERSIFIES After the decline of the copper industry, the Anaconda Copper Mining Company was bought by Atlantic Richfield Company in 1976. By 1983, when the copper mines had completely closed, unemployment in Butte rose to more than seventeen percent. The city lost 4,400 jobs, and many people moved away. Over time, however, Butte's city officials began to learn from past mistakes. As a result, they started to diversify (or vary) the local economy in an effort to save what was left of their town.

ness did not stop completely in Butte. Some companies just changed their mining techniques. Traditionally, in order to extract precious resources buried deep in the earth, miners dug a series of tunnels and shafts. Eventually Butte-based companies adopted another method, which involved simply digging a huge hole deep enough to strike minerals. Digging tunnels and shafts had been extremely hazardous to the environment, but gouging a gaping hole out of the earth caused even more widespread effects in the area. Many of Butte's historical buildings were torn down so that the mining hole, which was called the "Pit," could be placed in the middle of the city. By 1983 mining in the hole had ended. The Pit remained, however, as a symbol of the destruction in Butte.

An environmental disaster

By the time the Pit was closed, the damage had already been done. By the late 1990s Butte ranked as one of America's worst environmental disasters. After so many years of industry, the city was polluted by soot filled with arsenic (a poisonous element) and littered with broken-down mining equipment. City water was barely drinkable. The infamous Pit filled up with rainwater until it contained a lake that was 800 feet deep. Butte eventually became the biggest Superfund site in the country. The Superfund is a portion of the national budget supplied by taxes that is used to clean up dangerous sites. The fund was created in 1980 after the Love Canal (see "Science and Technology" entry) contamination that took place in New York state. The Environmental Protection Agency (EPA) planned to spend decades and billions of dollars to clean up Butte.

FOR FURTHER REFERENCE

Periodicals

Baum, Dan. "Butte, America: Poisoned, Ruined, and Self-cannibalized, This City is Still the Grandest of All Boomtowns." *American Heritage.* April 1997.

Dobb, Edwin. "Pennies from Hell: In Montana, the Bill for America's Copper Comes Due." *Harper's.* October 1997.

The Sinking of the *Titanic*

APRIL 14, 1912

Instead of becoming a symbol of the triumph of technology, the *Titanic* has gone down in history as an example of human misjudgment and overconfidence.

On the night of April 14, 1912, the ocean liner *Titanic* had nearly completed crossing the Atlantic on its maiden voyage from Southampton, England, to New York City. The largest and most luxurious vessel afloat in the early twentieth century, the *Titanic* approached the coast of Newfoundland around 9:00 P.M. Only two hours and forty minutes later, at 11:40 P.M., the ship hit an iceberg and began to sink, eventually taking more than fifteen hundred passengers to their deaths. The catastrophe was shocking, even unbelievable, because the *Titanic* had been promoted to potential passengers as being "practically unsinkable."

Instead of becoming a symbol of the triumph of technology, however, the *Titanic* has gone down in history as an example of human misjudgment and overconfidence. Many causes have been cited for the sinking, including errors on the part of the ship's captain, improper lifeboat procedures, mishaps in wireless radio communication, and structural weaknesses in the ship's steel plates. The *Titanic* disaster, with its great loss of life, eventually led to the creation of the International Ice Patrol for the monitoring of iceberg movement. Another result was the licensing of amateur wireless radio operators, which was the beginning of the Federal Communications Commission (FCC) in the United States.

Competition in the ocean liner industry

At the turn of the twentieth century, when ocean travel had reached its peak in popularity, steamship companies were engaged in an intense rivalry. The leader was the British-owned Cunard Line, which was noted for its high-speed vessels. In 1907 J. Bruce Ismay, chairman of the White Star Line (another British ship company), decided to build ocean liners that could successfully compete with Cunard. Ismay joined forces with William James Pirie, head of Harland & Wolff, a firm based in Belfast, Ireland, that was famous for constructing the sturdiest and best ships in the British Isles. Since Pirie and Ismay realized they could not surpass Cunard liners in speed, they decided to concentrate on size, safety, and luxury. With immigrant traffic on the rise, the two men also planned to provide better accommodations (or lodgings) for steerage passengers (customers who pay the lowest fares).

The *Titanic:* indestructible and luxurious

The first ships produced in the Ismay-Pirie venture were the *Titanic* and the *Olympic*. The ships were built alongside one another at the Harland & Wolff shipyards in Belfast. Although the *Olympic* was the longer of the two vessels, the *Titanic* was heavier. Measuring 882 feet in length and 92 feet in width, the ship weighed 46,328 tons. Its nine steel decks rose as high as an eleven-story building. The *Titanic's* vast size was considered one of the many safeguards against overturning or sinking. Another safety feature was the use of more steel in the outer structure than was customary in shipbuilding. Thus, the *Titanic* was constructed with a heavier and thicker bottom (the part of a ship's main body, or hull, lying below the water) that consisted of two skins (layers). The outer skin alone was a full inch thick.

To guard against flooding, the huge hull (main body) of the *Titanic* was divided by fifteen bulkheads (upright partitions that extend across the width of the hull). Rising from the double bottom to five decks above forward (the front of the ship) and aft (the back of the ship), and to four decks above amidships (the middle of the ship), the bulkheads formed sixteen watertight compartments. The theory of this design was that any two of the compartments could be flooded without affecting the safety of the ship. As an additional precaution, the six

compartments that contained boilers had their own pumping equipment. The doors between watertight compartments could be closed all at once by a switch on the bridge (the forward part of the ship that houses navigating instruments), or they could be secured individually by crewmen.

The *Titanic* was not only the biggest ship afloat, it was also the last word in comfort and elegance. Among the accommodations were the first shipboard swimming pool, a Turkish bath with a cooling room decorated in gold, a gymnasium, and a squash court. Additional innovations included a crane for loading baggage and cargo, a special compartment for automobiles, and a hospital with a modern operating room. The dining rooms, staterooms (private rooms), and common rooms were furnished in various styles and periods, featuring, for instance, a Parisian cafe. The first-class cabins were especially luxurious, with coal-burning fireplaces in the sitting rooms and full-size four-poster beds in the bedrooms.

Criticism of grandiose design

Possibly because the *Titanic* represented the overconfident spirit of the times, critics were reluctant to voice concern about the venture. Some dissenters, however, pointed out that there was no dock in the United States big enough for the *Titanic* or the *Olympic*. Others said that offering the height of luxury would increase the expense of ocean travel rather than produce more economical transportation. Still others concluded that the two ships, by virtue of their great size, would crowd too many passengers into a single vessel. Also there was serious concern that insurance companies would not be able to write policies to cover accidents or loss of life.

Captain is overconfident

The *Titanic* was launched from Belfast on May 31, 1911. Amid much celebration the ship set sail from Southampton, England, on April 9, 1912. With Captain E. J. Smith at the helm, the ship carried more than 2,200 passengers. On the evening of April 14—the fifth day into the trip across the Atlantic—the sea was exceptionally calm and the sky was star-

◄ Before its first voyage, the *Titanic* docked at the port in Southhampton, England.

The New York Times.

THE WEATHER.

VOL. LXI. NO. 19,806.

NEW YORK, TUESDAY, APRIL 16, 1912.—TWENTY-FOUR PAGES.

ONE CENT

TITANIC SINKS FOUR HOURS AFTER HITTING ICEBERG; 866 RESCUED BY CARPATHIA, PROBABLY 1250 PERISH; ISMAY SAFE, MRS. ASTOR MAYBE, NOTED NAMES MISSING

Col. Astor and Bride, Isidor Straus and Wife, and Maj. Butt Aboard.

"RULE OF SEA" FOLLOWED

Women and Children Put Over in Lifeboats and Are Supposed to be Safe on Carpathia.

PICKED UP AFTER 8 HOURS

Vincent Astor Calls at White Star Office for News of His Father and Leaves Weeping.

FRANKLIN HOPEFUL ALL DAY

Manager of the Line Insisted Titanic Was Unsinkable Even After She Had Gone Down.

HEAD OF THE LINE ABOARD

J. Bruce Ismay Making First Trip on Gigantic Ship That Was to Surpass All Others.

The Lost Titanic Being Towed Out of Belfast Harbor.

CAPT. E. J. SMITH, Commander of the Titanic.

Biggest Liner Plunges to the Bottom at 2:20 A. M.

RESCUERS THERE TOO LATE

Except to Pick Up the Few Hundreds Who Took to the Lifeboats.

WOMEN AND CHILDREN FIRST

Cunarder Carpathia Rushing to New York with the Survivors.

SEA SEARCH FOR OTHERS

The Californa Stands By on Chance of Picking Up Other Boats or Rafts.

OLYMPIC SENDS THE NEWS

Only Ship to Flash Wireless Messages to Shore After the Disaster.

LATER REPORT SAVES 866.

BOSTON, April 15.—A wireless message picked up late to-night, relayed from the Olympic, says that the Carpathia is on her way to New York with 866 passengers from the steamer Titanic aboard. They are mostly women and children, the message read, and it concluded "Grave fears are felt for the safety of the balance of the passengers and crew."

PARTIAL LIST OF THE SAVED.

Includes Bruce Ismay, Mrs. Widener, Mrs. H. B. Harris, and an Incomplete name, suggesting Mrs. Astor's.

ry but moonless. It was later revealed that Smith had received numerous warnings about ice in the seas around Newfoundland (an island off the eastern coast of Canada). Even if the captain had been given no warnings, however, he would have been expected to know that April is one of the worst months for icebergs. (An iceberg is a floating mass of ice that has broken off from a glacier, or larger body of ice.) Most icebergs come from the west coast of Greenland (an island located in the Arctic Circle). Each year about a thousand icebergs move into shipping routes, including the area where the *Titanic* was sailing. Although Smith is known to have sighted at least four ice fields (extensive sheets of ice in the water), he did not slow the speed of the ship. On the evening of April 14, the *Titanic* was traveling about 21 knots (nautical miles) per hour.

There are several probable reasons for Smith's course of action. Good visibility, coupled with the notion that the *Titanic* was unsinkable, must have made him confident that he could cope with the situation. Ice fields were a hazard the captain encountered all the time. Smith was probably trying to maintain top speed on the ship's maiden voyage because reaching his destination on time would ensure future business for the White Star Line.

Titanic crashes into iceberg

On the night of April 14, the two lookouts (crewmen who monitor the sea for potential hazards) on the *Titanic* were working without binoculars, which were supposed to be standard equipment on the White Star Line. As a result, they did not sight the iceberg until it was only a quarter mile away. Once the navigator (the person who steers the ship) was alerted, he swung the bow (the forward part of the ship) swiftly to port (left) in an effort to avoid a collision. It was too late. The underwater shelf of the ice tore through the bottom of the starboard (right) bow, puncturing six watertight compartments. As the bow started to sink, more compartments filled with water, which soon sloshed over the tops of the bulkheads.

Since the gigantic, 46,000-ton *Titanic* was traveling at 21 knots, the impact of the collision was scarcely felt. Although

◀ The headline on the front page of the *New York Times* offered information about the *Titanic* passengers who were saved, including Bruce Ismay, the chairman of the White Star Line.

the collision occurred at 11:40 P.M., the order to ready the lifeboats was not given until 12:20 A.M. It took the crew some time to comprehended the seriousness of the situation. Once they were aware of the emergency, crew members began to awaken the passengers, most of whom were not even aware of the incident.

Crew becomes confused

Mass confusion reigned as the crew scrambled to load passengers into lifeboats. The primary problem was that the *Titanic* contained only sixteen lifeboats and four emergency rafts—enough for roughly half of the boat's passengers. Although White Star had complied with British Board of Trade rules regarding lifeboats, the number of boats was based on the tonnage of the ship rather than on passenger capacity. The law also allowed a reduction in the number of boats for ships declared to have safe, watertight compartments—a much-praised feature of the *Titanic*.

Since there had been no practice drill for evacuating the ship, neither the crew nor the passengers knew which boats had been designated for which passengers. Furthermore, the officers in charge of evacuating the ship were afraid fully loaded lifeboats would buckle as they were being lowered, or the davits (cranes) holding the boats over the side would break. The officers were obviously unaware that the boats and davits had already been tested for safety. They decided the best way to avoid a catastrophe was to allow only a few passengers to get into the boats from the decks. In the meantime, other passengers would go down to the cargo ports (openings in the side of the ship used for loading freight), where the crew would pick them up in the boats. The cargo ports were never opened, however, so many boats went away only partly filled.

The *Titanic* sinks

As the *Titanic*'s bow sank lower and lower, passengers remaining on the ship climbed to the stern (the rear portion of the ship). Many ended up jumping into twenty-eight-degree Fahrenheit water in their life belts (life preservers in the form of an inflatable belt). As people in the lifeboats watched spellbound, the immense stern reared up at a nearly vertical angle

As the *Titanic* sank, mass confusion made proper loading of the ship's lifeboats impossible. As a result, many passengers ended up jumping into the frigid ocean in their life belts.

and remained still for a few moments. Then, at 2:20 A.M., the *Titanic* sank slowly into the sea. Many survivors reported hearing sounds like thunder, or a kind of "death rattle," before the ship disappeared under the waters.

Although some passengers claimed that the great ship broke in two, the explanation generally accepted for the thunderous sound was that, as the stern rose, the boilers crashed down through the bulkheads. From what is now known about the position of the bow and the stern on the ocean floor—they are facing in opposite directions about 1,970 feet apart—it seems likely that the ship did break in two at or near the surface. As the bow sank and the stern rose, the pressure on the keel (the supporting beam that runs the length of the bottom of a ship) probably increased until it snapped.

Radio operators miss distress call

It is also likely that mishaps in wireless radio communication contributed to further unnecessary loss of life on the *Titanic*. Another ship, the *Californian*, had stopped for the night in ice fields not more than twenty miles away. The wireless operator on the *Californian* had quit working only fifteen or twenty minutes before the operator from the *Titanic* tried to get through with a distress call. (At the time, wireless operators were employees of the Marconi company, a private firm, and were not required to follow around-the-clock shipboard watches.) The next closest ship—which the *Titanic* did succeed in reaching—was the *Carpathia,* about fifty-eight miles away. The *Carpathia* picked up the first *Titanic* lifeboat at 4:10 A.M., less than five hours after the collision.

New shipping rules and regulations

Following the *Titanic* disaster, both the United States and British governments held hearings to determine why a supposedly unsinkable vessel had broken up in the sea. A U.S. Senate inquiry was begun the day after the *Carpathia* landed in New York City with the *Titanic* survivors. A British investigation by the Board of Trade followed in May through July of 1912. An international Safety of Life at Sea (SOLAS) conference met in London, England, from November 1913 to January 1914.

Many new rules and regulations resulted from these and later forums. Among the measures was the requirement that the number of lifeboats on a ship be based on the number of passengers rather than on the tonnage of the ship. Another directive was that lifeboat drills be held soon after a ship sails, with crew members and passengers assigned a particular place in a boat. Training of seamen assigned to boats and installation of permanent equipment in the boats were also more closely regulated.

NEW LIGHT SHED ON TITANIC

Since the mid-1980s researchers have made many interesting discoveries about the sinking of the *Titanic*. In 1985 Dr. Robert D. Ballard organized Operation *Titanic* with a group of French scientists. Using the U.S. Navy research ship *Knorr* as its base, Ballard's expedition was able to photograph the wreck from numerous angles. Ballard observed many buckled plates below the waterline, but found no gash in the bow. A more thorough examination of the bow was made difficult, however, by thick layers of mud covering that area of the ship.

In 1993 a team of architects and engineers released a report that proposed the *Titanic* tragedy was caused in part by a structural weakness in the ship's steel plates. Low-grade steel—such as that used on the *Titanic* is subject to brittle fracture (breaking rather than bending in cold temperatures). If a higher grade of steel had been used, the ship's plates might have had the flexibility to withstand the collision.

Researchers on a 1996 French expedition suggested an additional factor in the *Titanic*'s destruction: faulty wrought iron rivets along the ship's steel plate seams. (A rivet is a metal bolt with a head on one end. On the *Titanic*, rivets were driven through the steel hull plates from the outside, then the headless ends were hammered down on the inside to make a tight fit.) Upon examination, several *Titanic* rivets showed signs of too much slag. (Slag is a compound made up of silicon, sand, and glass used in small amounts to strengthen iron. Too much slag can make iron very brittle.) Slag-heavy rivets would not have been able to hold the ship's seams together under the intense pressure of the incoming water.

According to researchers, there may never be a definitive explanation as to what finally caused the *Titanic*'s structure to fail. Records of the ship's construction have been lost, and it is still very difficult to get samples for study from the ocean floor. As long as questions about the sinking remain, however, there will be scientists looking for answers.

The *Titanic* tragedy produced permanent changes in ocean routes. Shipping lanes were moved farther south, away from the ice drifting off the Arctic Circle, and ships approaching ice fields were required to slow down or alter their course. The International Ice Patrol, based in Groton, Connecticut, was set up to monitor iceberg movement. Still operating today, the International Ice Patrol uses aircraft with side-looking radar to spot icebergs, making computerized predictions about their whereabouts. To date, no further loss of life has occurred as a result of collision with an iceberg in the North Atlantic shipping lanes monitored by this control.

New regulations were also instituted for wireless operations. A ship's radio must now be operated day and night, and a backup power source must be available. The interference of

A POPULAR TALE The story of the *Titanic*'s final voyage has been the subject of several movies, television dramas, documentaries, and a 1997 Broadway play. The most well-known film adaptations include *Titanic,* released in 1953 by Twentieth Century-Fox; *A Night to Remember,* a British production released in 1958 by J. Arthur Rank; and director James Cameron's 1997 blockbuster *Titanic,* which became one of the biggest box office successes of all time. Recent television adaptations include *S.O.S. Titanic,* presented by the American Broadcasting Company (ABC-TV) in 1979.

amateur wireless operators in the *Titanic* tragedy, mostly in the period after the sinking and before the survivors had been brought to shore, led to the licensing of all operators in the United States. This licensing marked the beginning of the FCC.

From a technological point of view, the biggest factors in the *Titanic* tragedy were the speed at which the ship sank and the bulkhead construction and reinforcement. After the sinking, ship captains were instructed to be very careful with speed in potentially dangerous waters. New bulkhead regulations led to the reconstruction of many passenger ships. Nevertheless, it is questionable how well many ships built today—even with high-grade steel construction—could withstand the kind of blow suffered by the *Titanic*.

FOR FURTHER REFERENCE

Books

Ballard, Robert D. *Discovery of the Titanic: Exploring the Greatest of All Lost Ships.* New York City: Warner Books, 1989.

Sloan, Frank, *Titanic.* New York: F. Watts, 1987.

Periodicals

Broad, William J., "Faulty Rivets Emerge as Clues To *Titanic* Disaster." *New York Times.* January 27, 1988, pp. B9, B13.

The Boston Molasses Spill

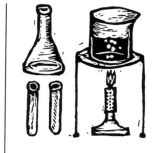

JANUARY 15, 1919

One of the most bizarre structural failures on record took place in the working-class North End of Boston, Massachusetts, on January 15, 1919. On that mild winter day, a steel tank containing nearly twelve thousand tons of thick, brown, sugary molasses burst open without warning. A massive tidal wave of molasses gushed from the fractured tank. The wave of molasses, which was 15 feet high and 160 feet wide, moved at a rate of thirty-five miles per hour, destroying everything in its path. The spill left twenty-one people dead, injured more than one hundred fifty others, and demolished many buildings. The tank that contained the molasses was the largest that the Hammond Iron Works had ever built. After six years of litigation (court trials) following the incident, the Massachusetts Supreme Court wrote a decision (or finding) that the tank was poorly constructed. As a result of the court's ruling, the Boston spill led to stricter regulations on building permits in Boston and across the country.

> The Boston molasses spill left twenty-one people dead, injured more than one hundred fifty others, and demolished many buildings.

Poor construction leads to tragedy

The tank that burst open on January 15 was doomed from the start. It was ordered from Hammond Iron Works in 1915 by the Purity Distilling Company on authorization of U.S. Industrial Alcohol. The treasurer of Purity Distilling, a man

On January 15, 1919, the rupture of a tank holding over two million gallons of molasses created widespread destruction in Boston's North End.

named Mr. Jell, ordered the tank without consulting an engineer. The only requirement for the tank was that it had to be safe enough for the storage of molasses weighing twelve pounds per gallon (fifty percent heavier than water).

The huge tank was fifty feet high and ninety feet in diameter. It was the largest tank that the Hammond Iron Works had ever built. According to the blueprints, the sides of the circular structure consisted of seven rings of steel sheets, each about seven feet high, varying in thickness from .687 inches at the bottom to .312 inches at the top. The flat bottom of the tank rested on a cement sand cushion, with a concrete slab foundation. This slab was supported on concrete piles. The roof of the tank, conical (like a cone) in shape, was made up of curved steel sheets supported by framing (or beam rafters).

Unfortunately, the tank was not built according to the blueprints. All the steel sheets used in constructing the tank were actually less thick than shown on the Hammond drawings. The bottom ring—the most stressed part of the structure—was supposed to be .687 inches thick. The ring used in construction measured only .667 inches. The steel thickness for the other six rings was also five to ten percent less than shown on the permit plans. The bottom ring even had a twenty-one-inch manhole opening cut out of it, a factor that added to the weakness of the structure.

The weakest elements of the tank's construction were its rivets, bolts, and welds. (A rivet is a metal bolt with a head on one end. In sheet metal construction, rivets are driven through the metal from the outside, then the headless ends are hammered down on the inside to make a tight fit. A weld is formed by heating metal until it is soft enough to hammer or press together.) The steel sheets that made up the rings were joined together in two ways. The sheets in the bottom rings had butt joints and splice plates. (A butt joint is made by fastening the parts together end-to-end without overlap. A splice plate reinforces a butt joint by lapping the two ends together). The sheets in the other six rings had lap joints. Both types of joints were riveted together with six rows of rivets—three on each side of the joints. The rings were connected to each other by a lap joint using a single row of rivets.

Tank bursts

The tank was completed in early 1916 and tested only to a fill-depth of six inches. The tank loomed above and was sandwiched between several buildings, including a freight depot, a firehouse, stables, offices, and even an elevated railway. On twelve occasions during its three years of service, the tank contained a maximum of around 1.9 million gallons of molasses for periods of up to twenty-five days. The contents on January

AN EYEWITNESS ACCOUNT

Boston newspaperman Ralph Frye filed an eyewitness report about the molasses spill for *The Boston American.* In his account, Frye describes the wave as looking like a "moving wall of volcanic lava" swallowing up everything in its path. People and animals lost their lives in the catastrophe, either by drowning or by being struck by wreckage.

Several horses had to be shot. Occupied houses were demolished, while the cellars of others were filled with molasses. Horse-drawn and motor vehicles were marooned or floated away. Rescue crews found one man and his wagon embedded in a mountain of molasses, the man and his horse both frozen in motion.

15 was about 2.3 million gallons—a near-capacity amount—and the molasses had been in the tank for four days. Months later several witnesses recalled that the seams of the tank were leaking molasses, but no one at Hammond or Purity Distilling seemed to be concerned.

At 12:40 P.M., eyewitnesses said they heard sounds like machine-gun fire, then saw a wall of molasses two stories high exploding out from the tank. A 2.5-ton section of the lower part of the tank was pushed out onto a playground 182 feet away. Another section of the structure wrapped itself around and completely sheared off one column of an adjacent elevated railway. Traveling at about thirty-five miles per hour, the molasses swept over and through everything in its path. At its most destructive moments, the wave was 15 feet high and 160 feet wide.

By midafternoon the flood had settled. The wave remains covered more than a two-block area that looked like it had been hit by a cyclone. Buildings were destroyed or bulldozed off their foundations, rails from the elevated railway were dangling in the air, and the tank itself lay on the ground, a heap of crumbled junk metal. Police and firemen used huge hydraulic siphons around the clock to pump molasses out of flooded cellars. It was nearly a week before all the bodies were recovered.

Court gives its decision

There were numerous lawsuits as a result of the spill. More than three thousand witnesses appeared before the Massachusetts Supreme Court, offering 6 million words of testimony that filled 40,000 pages of court records. During the trial, the Purity Distilling Company suggested three likely causes for the failure: an explosion, train vibrations on the adjacent elevated track, and the collision of a runaway trolley freight car. The explosion theory got the most attention, but in the long run all three factors were easily dismissed as the cause of the spill. After nearly six years of litigation, the Massachusetts Supreme Court declared that the tank was improperly designed, detailed, and constructed. The court also noted that the tank's structure-stress calculations were never checked by an experienced engineer. When all the court cases were complete, the total claim settlement for damages exceeded $1 million (a large amount of money in 1925).

Stricter regulations imposed

Immediately after the event, the Boston Building Department began requiring that all design calculations (such as required metal thickness) be filed with the engineering plans. The department also demanded that all stamped blueprint drawings be signed. The catastrophe probably influenced the adoption of engineering certification laws in all states that did not already have such legislation. It also helped pave the way for the requirement that all plans for major structures be approved by a registered professional engineer before issuance of a building permit.

The Boston molasses spill was largely the result of overconfidence and neglect. Improperly placed joints, the existence of a manhole, and the use of thin steel sheets were all factors in the tank's failure. Because of the incident's casualty counts and damage costs, the spill highlighted the need for vigilance, not only in building construction and maintenance, but in the choice of structure location as well.

FOR FURTHER REFERENCE

Periodicals

Bluthardt, Robert. "Wave of Death." *Firehouse.* June 1983, pp. 86–88, 136.

The Failure of the Artificial Heart

1935 TO 1990

In 1990 the Food and Drug Administration withdrew approval for the experimental use of the Jarvik-7 artificial heart.

The development of the artificial heart is a story of both hope and failure. Scientists have long been fascinated with the idea of making a machine that could function like the human heart. The ultimate challenge was to design an artificial heart that could be permanently implanted, or placed, in the human body. Medical researchers achieved this goal when a device called the "Jarvik-7" was implanted in Indianapolis dentist Barney Clark in 1982. Invented by American physician and biomedical engineer Robert Jarvik, the Jarvik-7 functioned for 112 days. After the failure of several other implantation surgeries, however, the U.S. Food and Drug Administration withdrew approval of experimental use of the Jarvik-7.

Early heart pumps

Since the heart functions as a pump that circulates blood through the body, medical researchers have long considered developing a mechanical pump to replace the heart in the case of a malfunction or disease. Building an artificial replacement, however, was not easy. Early attempts at designing an artificial heart were not very successful. For instance, in 1935 French surgeon Alexis Carrel (1873–1944) and famed American aviator Charles Lindbergh (1902-1974) designed a perfusion pump. Instead of being implanted in the human body, the perfusion pump was designed to work outside the human body. Its job was to keep unattached organs, including the heart, alive by circulating blood through them.

Over the course of time, artificial heart surgery became more sophisticated. Doctors even started implanting the devices into the human body. The first completely artificial heart (called "TAH") was implanted in 1957 in a dog at the Cleveland Clinic. The surgery was performed by a team headed by Dutch-born surgeon Willem Kolff (1911–), who later became an important figure in the implantation field. During the 1960s, artificial heart research broke new ground. In 1964 the National Institutes of Health established an Artificial Heart Program to develop both partial and total artificial heart devices. American surgeon and inventor Michael DeBakey (1908–) designed and implanted a pneumatically-driven (worked by air pressure) component called a "Left Ventricular Assist Device" (LVAD) in 1966.

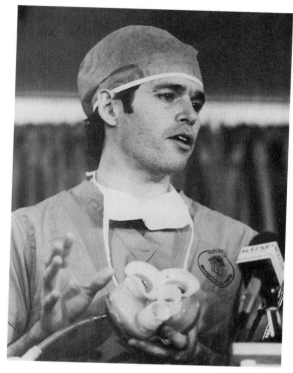

By the early 1980s Dr. Robert K. Jarvik had developed an artificial heart that could be implanted in a human being.

First implantation

The first implantation of an artificial heart in a human being was finally carried out in 1969. Denton Cooley (1920–) and his surgical team at the Texas Heart Institute performed the surgery. The pneumatically driven, Dacron-lined plastic heart used in the procedure was designed by Argentine-born inventor Domingo Liotta. Implanted as a temporary measure, the plastic heart's goal was to keep a cardiac patient alive until a heart transplant (the insertion of a heart from one human to the body of another) could be performed.

Advances in research

Artificial heart research reached its peak during the 1970s and 1980s with breakthrough work by Kolff at the University of Utah Institute of Biomedical Research. Having successfully implanted an artificial heart in a dog in 1957, Kolff became the

ROBERT K. JARVIK Robert Koffler Jarvik (1946–) was born in Midland, Michigan, the son of physician Norman Eugene Jarvik and Edythe Koffler Jarvik. Robert was raised in Stamford, Connecticut, where he spent a lot of time inventing gadgets. He often watched his father performing surgery; in fact, even before he graduated from high school Jarvik had invented an automatic surgical stapler. The device was designed to replace the process of manually sewing up living body tissue.

Jarvik entered Syracuse University in 1964 and took courses in mechanical drawing and architecture. His father's heart disease, however, prompted him to change his course of study. Jarvik began premedical course work, graduating in 1968 with a bachelor's degree in zoology. His immediate plans were stalled when only average grades prevented him from gaining acceptance into an American medical school. As an alternative he attended medical school at the University of Bologna in Italy. After two years he returned to the United States to pursue a degree in occupational biomechanics (the study of the mechanics of biological processes such as muscular activity) at New York University, receiving a master's degree in 1971. In 1976, while working at the University of Utah Institute of Biomedical Research, Jarvik earned a medical degree from the University of Utah.

leader of a large-scale and complex medical project that had the full institutional support of the University of Utah.

Creating an artificial heart with a suitable power source was the major obstacle facing Kolff's team. The team members concluded that the ideal solution was a single unit containing both the pump and a power source that would be completely encased in the recipient's body. Kolff worked hard to create an electrical power source. After that failed, he developed a nuclear-powered source. When this strategy also failed, Kolff decided to concentrate on perfecting a pump powered by compressed air from a machine that remained outside the body and was connected by tubes to the artificial heart. Scientifically, the decision was sound, as it divided a complex problem into two simpler parts. In actual practice, however, it meant that the recipient of the artificial heart would be permanently attached by tubes to a machine.

Jarvik makes further strides

Probably the most important figure in the history of artificial heart research was Jarvik. Jarvik was hired by the University of Utah Institute of Biomedical Research after he had received a master's degree in occupational biomechanics in 1971. His achievements in biomedical engineering were closely tied to his employment at the well-funded institute under Kolff, who was an expert on man-made organs. Jarvik's inventive genius soon solved several problems associated with the devices. By the early 1980s, Jarvik had developed an artificial heart that could be implanted in a human being.

When Jarvik arrived at the institute, he immediately began working on the "Kwann-Gett heart," which was designed in 1971 by a member of Kolff's team named Clifford S. Kwann-Gett. This device used a rubber diaphragm as the pumping element that forced blood in and out of the artificial heart. The diaphragm represented an improvement in that it lowered the possibility of mechanical failure. It also, however, caused blood to clot on its surface, which could lead to death. Jarvik's improved version, called the "Jarvik-3," was shaped to better fit the anatomy of experimental animals. In addition, the rubber of the Jarvik-3's diaphragm had been replaced by three highly flexible layers of a smooth polyurethane (a kind of plastic) called "biomer," which eliminated the clotting problem.

Jarvik-7 implanted in Clark

By the mid-1970s, Jarvik was working on the latest refinement of the "Jarvik" series, an artificial heart called the Jarvik-7. This plastic and aluminum device replaced the lower pumping chambers of the heart (the ventricles) and was attached to the two upper chambers (the atria), which receive blood from the veins. The compressed air was delivered by a large external air compressor through two tubes that passed into the body via incisions in the abdomen.

Barney B. Clark (1921–1983), a sixty-one-year-old retired dentist, became the first recipient of the Jarvik-7, on December 2, 1982. Suffering from a terminal (deadly) illness, Clark believed that the experimental surgery could extend his life and contribute to the progress of medical science. A team headed by surgeon William C. Devries, with assistance from Jarvik, performed the procedure at the University of Utah.

The surgery received worldwide publicity. Shortly after the operation, however, Clark suffered from a series of disabling brain seizures. He survived for only 112 days, and died on

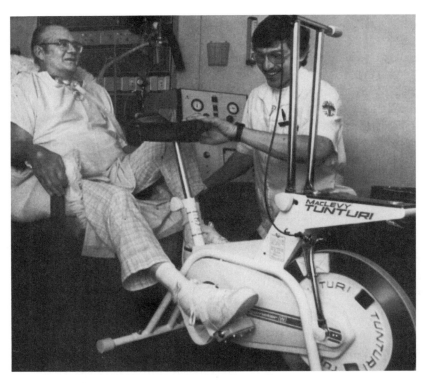

Barney Clark (left) rides an exercycle during his recovery from implantation surgery.

March 23, 1983. The artificial heart itself (except for a malfunctioning valve, which was replaced) functioned throughout Clark's illness and was still pumping when the patient died of multiple organ failure.

Further ventures fail

By the time the Jarvik-7 was implanted in Clark, Jarvik had left the Institute of Biomedical Research and joined Symbion, Inc. (originally Kolff Associates), an artificial organs research firm founded by Kolff. Jarvik was appointed president of the company in 1981. Seeking capital (or money), he arranged an independent deal with an outside investment firm. Under the terms of the agreement, however, Kolff was deliberately excluded from direct involvement in Symbion. This move became a source of friction between Jarvik and Kolff, although they reportedly cooperated in developing and manufacturing other artificial organs, including an ear.

After Clark's surgery Devries joined the staff at Humana Hospital in Louisville, Kentucky. At Humana he carried out four other Jarvik-7 implants during 1984 and 1985. Each of Devries's patients died. One of these patients was William Schroeder, who survived 620 days but suffered a long series of debilitating setbacks during that period. The results of actual permanent implantation of the Jarvik-7 revealed its limitations, including the fact that it caused blood clots to form that traveled to the brain and caused strokes. The Jarvik-7 therefore was frequently and more successfully used as a temporary measure for patients awaiting a natural heart transplant.

FDA halts implantations

After Jarvik's departure from the both the University of Utah and Symbion in 1987, the Jarvik-7 artificial heart did not fare well. Federal funding for the Jarvik project stopped in 1988, and further artificial heart implantation was restricted to temporary use only. In 1990 the Food and Drug Administration (FDA) withdrew approval for the experimental use of the Jarvik-7, citing Symbion's poor quality control in the manufacturing process and inadequate service of equipment. Although Jarvik formed his own company in 1987 and was reportedly working on the Jarvik 2000, there have been no other experimental implantations of an artificial heart.

FOR FURTHER REFERENCE

Books

Berger, Melvin. *The Artificial Heart*. New York City: F. Watts, 1987.

The *Hindenburg* Airship Crash

MAY 6, 1937

The crash of the *Hindenburg* resulted in the end of airship travel throughout the world.

On May 6, 1937, the *Hindenburg,* the largest airship ever built, had just completed a flight across the Atlantic Ocean. As the ship prepared to land at Lakehurst, New Jersey, the *Hindenburg* air crew dropped rope mooring (anchoring) lines to the ground crew below. Without warning, the giant German airship suddenly exploded and burst into flames. Thirty-two seconds later, the remains of the craft lay crumpled on the ground. Of the ninety-seven passengers and flight crew on board, sixty-two people survived the wreck. The reasons for the May 6 crash remain a mystery, especially since the airship had been very dependable during previous flights. Two possible explanations for the disaster are sabotage (the intentional destruction of a machine or mechanism) or natural causes. No matter what the cause, however, the crash of the *Hindenburg* resulted in the end of airship travel throughout the world.

The greatest airship ever built

Since the end of World War I (1914–18), German designer Hugo Eckener (1868–1954) had dreamed of building the perfect airship, a craft of unparalleled size, speed, and comfort which would also be safe and profitable. (An airship consists of a cigar-shaped balloon filled with lighter-than-air gas, below which is attached a cabin that houses propeller-driven

The *Hindenburg* in flight over New York City. The airship's designer, Hugo Eckener, had dreamed of building a craft of unparalleled size, speed, comfort, and safety.

engines.) As head of the Zeppelin Company, the foremost manufacturer of airships, Eckener hoped to establish regular commercial airship flights across the Atlantic Ocean. Although the company's *Graf Zeppelin* airship had braved the Atlantic several times, Eckener envisioned a ship that was big enough and fast enough to maintain a regular schedule of rigorous long-distance flights across the ocean.

Germany has flawless record

During the early years of the twentieth century, many countries experimented with airship travel. No country was as successful as Germany. In fact, every country except Germany had suffered disastrous and humiliating fatal crashes. Not only were the Germans uniquely untouched by serious accidents, but their record in commercial airship flying was completely spotless—there had never been a passenger fatality on any German ship. The *Graf Zeppelin* alone had flown more than one million miles in passenger service without serious incident. By the end of 1934, when Eckener was about to begin construction of his new airship, every major nation that had an airship program had abandoned it or was about to do so.

The luxury of an ocean liner

The new airship showed promise of fulfilling Eckener's dream. At first designated the *LZ 129*, the ship was later christened the *Hindenburg* in honor of Germany's respected war hero and president, Field Marshal Paul von Hindenburg (1874–1934). The ship's dominant feature was its immense size—803 feet in length (29 feet longer than the old *Graf Zeppelin*) and 135 feet in diameter. The *Hindenburg* held nearly twice as much gas for greater lifting power, yet it was more resistant to bending forces and was considered more efficient. The airship also offered the latest technological innovations. Among these enhancements were four lightweight, eleven-hundred-horsepower Daimler-Benz diesel engines, which turned enormous reversible propellers that could drive the ship to a speed of more than eighty-five miles per hour.

Eckener was not only trying to build the ultimate airship; he was also competing with the ocean liner industry, which was booming at the turn of the century. He designed the *Hindenburg* so that the airship's traveling time would be far less than that of any ocean liner. Passengers would not have to give up any of the luxuries normally found on a boat, since the *Hindenburg* was a flying luxury liner. For a one-way fare of four hundred dollars, a passenger could enjoy a comfortable private cabin with hot and cold running water. The airship's fifty-foot-long dining room boasted an adjoining fifty-foot promenade deck with wide, sloping picture windows. The lounge on the starboard (right) side was thirty-four feet long and was furnished with tables and comfortable upholstered chairs. Elsewhere, passengers could find a writing room, another promenade deck, and spacious washrooms and showers. Smokers had a separate room that was sealed and protected by pressurization and an airlock. (This was a safety measure to avoid accidentally igniting the gas that held the airship aloft.) Passengers could not bring matches aboard the craft, so the smoker's room had an electric lighter secured by a chain for lighting cigarettes.

Hindered by politics

As the *Hindenburg* neared completion, Eckener encountered major obstacles in building his perfect airship. He had designed the craft to be lifted by helium, but he was forced to use hydrogen—a highly flammable gas—when the United States refused to sell scarce helium to Germany. The United States suspected that Germany, which had flown airships in bombing raids during World War I, might one day use helium-filled airships for military purposes. Another problem was that the popular Eckener was an anti-Nazi. (Naziism was the doctrine of the National Socialist Workers Party, which believed in totalitarian government rule, racial purity, and complete allegiance to chancellor Adolf Hitler.) Recognizing this fact, Adolf Hitler (1889–1945) had Eckener moved into the essentially powerless position of chairman of the board of the Zeppelin Company. The Nazi government then took over half ownership of the firm.

The *Hindenburg*'s maiden (first) flight, on March 4, 1936, was essentially a propaganda mission. For four days and three nights the airship was used by Nazi officials to broadcast speeches and drop leaflets promoting Hitler's policies. The *Hindenburg* made its first commercial flight on a March 31 trip to Rio de Janeiro, Brazil, carrying thirty-seven passengers. Eckener was unhappy about this long-distance flight, however, because the propaganda missions had made it impossible to conduct preliminary test trials. Although the *Hindenburg* landed safely in Rio, on the way back two of the Daimler engines failed and the ship barely completed the trip to Frankfurt, Germany. Repairs took a month to complete.

Comes to America

In February 1936, Germany obtained permission from the United States for the *Hindenburg* to make ten round trips to Lakehurst, New Jersey, during that year. The first flight took two and a half days, while the return trip was only two days, one hour, and fourteen minutes. In 1936 the *Hindenburg* completed the American trips plus six more to Rio de Janeiro, carrying more than fifteen hundred transatlantic passengers and twenty tons of mail and freight. Accommodations were plush, the meals were lavish, and no one ever got seasick. The airship completed all these early flights on schedule without difficulty.

A MYSTERIOUS DISASTER

More than any other airship disaster, the *Hindenburg* crash remains the most mysterious and most controversial. There are many explanations as to what caused the airship to suddenly catch fire, but over the years those explanations have narrowed down to one major theory: ignition of hydrogen by sabotage or by natural source, such as a spark of electricity. Investigations by both the German and American governments yielded no evidence of sabotage. Some critics have argued, however, that it was in the interest of both countries to suppress any embarrassing hint of foul play. A book published in 1962 called *Who Destroyed the Hindenburg?* even gave the name of the individual on board the airship who supposedly caused the crash. To this day, however, there has been no conclusive proof that the *Hindenburg* was sabotaged.

The *Hindenburg* proved to be amazingly stable. Gale force winds did not seem to affect the ship—in fact, it weathered a hurricane without the passengers being aware that they were flying through a serious storm. By year's end airship travel had won enthusiastic public endorsement. Prospects for the future of the airship seemed so bright that a German-American international company was formed with plans to put four Zeppelins—including the *Hindenburg's* sister ship, the *LZ 130*—into weekly service across the Atlantic. It appeared that Eckener's dream of a perfect airship had finally been realized.

The 1937 flying season for the *Hindenburg* began in March with the first of twenty flights to Rio de Janeiro. The United States had agreed to a May-through-November schedule of eighteen round-trips between Frankfurt and Lakehurst. The first *Hindenburg* flight to the United States was scheduled for a May 3 departure. Despite previous sold-out bookings, the passenger list totaled only thirty-six people. The rest of the seats were used for an unusually large group of German military officers and trainees.

Begins fateful voyage

Max Pruss, a former captain of the *Graf Zeppelin*, was in command as the *Hindenburg* cast off at 8:15 P.M. on May 3, 1937, from the newly completed Rhein-Main World Airport near Frankfurt. Heading north, the airship reached a cruising speed of nearly ninety miles per hour, but encountered a strong headwind off the coast of Ireland. For political reasons the ship could not fly over France or England, so it reached the North Atlantic by flying over the Netherlands, then coming down the English Channel. The arrival time at Lakehurst was scheduled for 6:00 A.M. on May 6, but with speed cut to sixty miles per hour by headwinds, landing on time looked impossible. Even further delays occurred as the weather deteriorated around Newfoundland and the ship's speed was reduced to only thirty-seven miles per hour. When the *Hindenburg* approached the New England coast of the United States, it was twelve hours behind schedule.

The *Hindenburg* flew over New York City at 3:00 P.M. The crew had been advised of an approaching cold front, however, so they kept the ship hovering in a holding pattern along the coast. During the next four hours the cold front was followed by heavy showers and a thunderstorm. By 7:00 P.M. conditions had improved, and the Lakehurst ground control crew finally told the *Hindenburg* to come in.

Prepares for mooring

At 7:08 P.M., the *Hindenburg* emerged from the clouds over Lakehurst, roaring at full speed at an altitude of 650 feet. The gigantic airship was an impressive sight for spectators as it passed over the field and made a sweeping turn to the left in order to approach the mooring mast (the structure to which to airship would be tied in order to secure it on the ground) from the west. As the airship returned over the field at 7:10 P.M., shifting winds forced Pruss to make another, much sharper turn to the right for a northerly approach instead. With the cloud ceiling between 2,000 and 3,000 feet, and a light rain falling, lightning flashed in the distant south and southwest. Pruss valved off (released with a valve) some hydrogen, which lowered the ship a bit. He also dropped some water ballast (water-filled containers used to give the ship stability). By maneuvering the four engines, he skillfully brought the huge ship to a complete stop in midair at 7:20 P.M.

Hindenburg explodes

At 7:21 P.M., the *Hindenburg* hovered at an altitude of about 200 feet, approximately 700 feet away from the mooring mast.

From the time the first flame was noticed until the *Hindenburg* lay smoldering on the ground, only thirty-two seconds had elapsed.

Crewmen first dropped the starboard (right) rope handling lines for the ground crew and then the port (left) lines. (Handling lines were ropes attached to the airship that were fastened to lines on the mooring mast.) The landing was proceeding normally as the ground crew continued to couple (or attach) the manila (a kind of hemp) rope lines to the corresponding lines on the ground. Then, as the ship was hovering

| Great Misadventures

between 135 and 150 feet, its outer cover began to flutter and its skin seemed to be rippling. About fifteen seconds later—at 7:25 P.M.—a small tongue of flame emerged from the place where the skin had been fluttering. In the control car, the crew felt a shudder in the ship's frame. At the same time, one of the crew in another part of the ship heard a muffled pop like a gas burner igniting on a stove.

Within seconds, all of these subtle disturbances were followed by a burst of exploding, flaming hydrogen that blasted from the top, just forward of the upper fin (a movable panel attached to the airship for directional stability). In a few more seconds, almost the entire stern (rear portion) of the ship was engulfed in flames and began to drop. Inside the control car, Pruss reached instinctively to drop the ballast and raise the ship, but instead made the split-second decision to let the ship's tail section crash to the ground. (Pruss knew this was the only hope of anyone possibly scrambling out alive.) As the great ship's tail dropped to the ground, its nose pointed skyward. Fire spread swiftly upward through the promenades, which served as chimneys. According to witnesses, flames shot out the nose of the airship "as from a blowtorch." Once this happened, the entire ship was engulfed and the framework quickly collapsed. From the time the first flame was noticed until the craft lay smoldering on the ground, only thirty-two seconds had elapsed.

The inferno killed thirteen passengers, twenty-two crewmen, and one civilian rope handler on the ground. Life or death was simply a matter of chance. Some men in the tail walked out virtually untouched as the flames in that section went upward. A cabin boy was saved when doused by ballast water. An acrobat used his professional skills to hang from a window as the ship fell, letting go at a safe height. Other people were saved by the heroic actions of the American ground crew. Captain Pruss refused to leave the burning ship and went back several times to help survivors get out. The flames of the *Hindenburg* continued for three hours amidst the chaos on the Lakehurst landing field.

Disaster investigated

In the wake of the disaster both the German and American governments sponsored investigations. After considering the possibility of sabotage, both teams of experts concluded that the airship's hydrogen was probably ignited by some type of atmospheric electrical discharge. The Americans argued that St. Elmo's Fire ignited the hydrogen. (St. Elmo's Fire is a discharge of electricity that sometimes occurs as an eerie bluish glow on the prominent parts of a ship or aircraft in stormy weather.) The Germans concluded that the manila ropes that were dropped to the ground became wet, resulting in the airship's "becoming a piece of ground elevated into the atmosphere." This equalization of the static charges between the ship and the ground meant that the *Hindenburg* would itself discharge electricity into the atmosphere, a phenomenon known as "brush discharge."

Each natural-cause argument was based on the assumption that hydrogen had been released from the ship and then was ignited. The fluttering cover was cited as an indicator that hydrogen was escaping. Bolstering this observation was the ship's tail-heaviness, which was witnessed by most spectators just before the explosion. Lack of lift may also have indicated a possible hydrogen loss. The final, official judgment was that the *Hindenburg* was destroyed accidentally by unusual, but natural, causes. Eckener agreed with this verdict, but Pruss argued for sabotage.

A recent bit of information supports the natural-cause argument. Records indicate that the *Hindenburg* had been painted with a different type of aircraft dope (a substance used to prepare the surface for painting). The theory is that the new dope ultimately helped create the deadly spark.

The end of airship travel

At the time of the *Hindenburg* crash, the German airship *Graf Zeppelin* was flying back from Rio de Janeiro. Upon its arrival in Germany, the *Graf Zeppelin* was grounded until the cause of the *Hindenburg* crash was determined. No zeppelin ever made another flight. The *Hindenburg* disaster not only resulted in the banning of hydrogen as a lifting medium for lighter-than-air craft but it also brought an end to airship travel. Despite the fact that for more than a quarter century commercial zeppelins had carried fifty thousand passengers without a fatality, airship travel was now considered unsafe.

Modern broadcasting media were largely responsible for this perception of danger. The *Hindenburg* catastrophe was the most thoroughly documented event of its kind at the time. The sights and sounds of May 6 were graphically captured on film, then shown over and over again on newsreels in movie theaters throughout the world. Equally dramatic was the heartbreaking, raw emotion of a live radio report by newsman Herb Morrison. As he helplessly watched the airship burn, Morrison cried, "Oh, the humanity and all the passengers!"

The spectacular crash of the *Hindenburg* had an impact on public opinion that far exceeded the fatality count. Despite the fact that nearly two-thirds of the people on board the airship survived, the name *Hindenburg* became forever linked with tragedy and sudden, terrifying technological failure. Long-distance air travel was not dead, however. Two years after the *Hindenburg*'s last flight, an airplane carried the first paying passenger across the Atlantic.

FOR FURTHER REFERENCE

Books

Hoehling, Adolph A. *Who Destroyed the Hindenburg?* New York City: Little, Brown, 1962.

Payne, Lee. *Lighter Than Air: An Illustrated History of the Airship.* New York City: Orion Books, 1991, pp. 218–29.

DDT Contamination

1939 TO PRESENT

The long-range effects of DDT exposure have not yet been determined. Scientists estimate that this toxic compound may have infiltrated the entire ecosystem of the Earth.

Widespread use of DDT has become one of the most disastrous environmental misadventures in history. (DDT is the popular name for the chemical compound dichloro diphenyl trichloroethane.) The chemical was widely used as an insecticide from the beginning of World War II (1939–45) until the early 1970s. Enthusiastically promoted by chemical companies, DDT was used to combat insects that spread typhus (an infectious disease carried by ticks and lice) and other diseases. It was also used by farmers and gardeners to control unwanted pests. American environmentalist Rachel Carson (1907–1964) was primarily responsible for raising public consciousness about insecticides such as DDT with the publication of her book *Silent Spring* in 1962. According to Carson, these chemicals were destroying the environment and the world was teetering on the edge of a monumental environmental catastrophe.

Carson criticized the perception of DDT and other pesticides as wonderful new weapons in the war against insects that destroy crops and cause disease. She revealed that, because of its prolonged toxicity (poisonous quality), DDT can contaminate the entire food chain, destroying plant, aquatic, bird, animal—even human— life. In the face of strong resistance from chemical manufacturers and federal policymakers, civic

A fogger spreads the pesticide DDT through a residential neighborhood in 1949.

activists filed lawsuits that led to the formation of the U.S. Environmental Protection Agency (EPA) in 1970. Eventually, most DDT use in the United States was banned. The chemical is still used in many countries, however, including Mexico.

DDT used throughout the world

DDT was first synthesized (chemically manufactured) in 1874 by German chemist Othmar Zeidler. In 1939 Swiss scientist Paul Müller discovered the insecticidal (insect-killing) properties of DDT. Müller received the 1946 Nobel Prize in Medicine for his discovery of the chemical's effectiveness in controlling insect-borne human diseases. DDT was used extensively and successfully during World War II to eliminate insect populations carrying typhus and malaria. It was also useful in preventing yellow fever (a destructive infectious disease of warm regions), river blindness (a disease caused by worms and black flies in tropical regions), elephantiasis (a thickening of

BOOK RAISES CONSCIOUSNESS The publication of Rachel Carson's book *Silent Spring* in 1962 was largely responsible for alerting the public to the widespread ecological threat posed by DDT. Born in 1907, Carson attended the Pennsylvania State College for Women. She later earned a master's degree in biology from Johns Hopkins University in Baltimore, Maryland. Carson taught at Johns Hopkins and the University of Maryland before taking a position with the U.S. Bureau of Fisheries (which later became the U.S. Fish and Wildlife Service) in 1936. A respected scientist and author, Carson wrote two books about the ocean and shore life before her publication of *Silent Spring*.

tissues caused by worms), and bubonic plague (a swelling of lymph glands caused by a virus).

After World War II, the chemical was primarily used for agricultural purposes. Before DDT became available, farmers and gardeners had used arsenicals (compounds containing arsenic, a highly poisonous chemical) to control pests such as beetles, moths, lice, butterflies, flies, and mosquitoes. Since arsenicals are costly to manufacture, DDT, which acts as a nerve gas on insects, was both cheaper and more effective. By 1959 124 million pounds of the pesticide were being manufactured annually for disease control, agriculture, gardening, and animal husbandry (the raising of animals). DDT was used throughout the world, but most heavily in tropical zones.

Carson exposes DDT disaster

In 1962 Carson published *Silent Spring,* which exposed the disastrous environmental effects of DDT. Contending that all life on earth is interrelated, Carson showed that polluting the ecosphere (parts of the universe habitable by living organisms) with pesticides or other toxic compounds results in unintended and unforeseeable consequences. *Silent Spring* documented the effects of DDT and other pesticides in reducing the populations of birds, fish, and certain mammals when indiscriminately applied to control specific insects. Carson did not denounce all use of pesticides, but rather advocated the selective use of these agents based on a full understanding of the consequences of their use.

Silent Spring dramatically portrays the destructiveness of pesticides. In chapters with such titles as "A Fable for

Two scientists test DDT levels in an artificial pond. Environmental scientists fear that the ecosystem contains many toxic compounds that may affect organisms in yet-unknown ways.

Tomorrow" and "And No Birds Sing," Carson depicts a world with no birds, fish, or wild animals. As an example of the deadly effects of DDT, she examines the common practice of spraying elm trees with DDT to slow the destruction of Dutch elm disease (a disease caused by fungus). Earthworms living underneath the trees ingest the DDT-poisoned leaves that fall to the ground. Robins feed on the earthworms. The robins then become sterile (infertile) or die from the poison, resulting in a rapid reduction in their numbers. In "The Other Road," the final chapter of *Silent Spring,* Carson discusses the use of alternative pest control methods, such as predator insects, bacteria, sterilants (agents that cause sterility), crop rotation, and ecological biodiversity (allowing many plants and animals to interact).

Although naturalists in the United States had noticed a reduction in the local bird population, most did not suspect the cause until Carson wrote *Silent Spring.* Concerned about the environmental effects of pesticides, citizens turned to the legal system, the U.S. Congress, and the executive branch of the federal government to force a reevaluation of pesticide use.

EPA is created

In 1962, the year *Silent Spring* was published, President John F. Kennedy, Secretary of Agriculture Orville Freeman, and Secretary of the Interior Stewart Udall addressed the issue of ecological hazards posed by pesticide use. The men's purpose was to weigh benefits in agricultural productivity against large-scale environmental contamination. Many members of the agriculture and the interior departments, however, resisted attempts to reevaluate or restrict the usage of DDT and other pesticides. Several of these federal employees had close alliances with the pesticide manufacturers, who aggressively attacked Carson and other ecological "fanatics."

In 1964 Congress acted to amend (revise) the Federal Insecticide, Fungicide, and Rodenticide Act (FIFRA) by tightening label guidelines and requiring that safety information be provided. In 1970 President Richard M. Nixon created the Environmental Protection Agency (EPA), which consolidated the major programs and agencies that dealt with environmental pollution. The EPA was authorized to regulate the introduction of new agricultural chemicals and other compounds into the marketplace, establishing safety guidelines and testing procedures.

DDT is banned

In 1969, a year before the EPA was established, federal regulations had begun phasing out the use of DDT. At the end of 1972, EPA administrator W. D. Ruckelshaus announced a ban on almost all uses of the toxic compound. Citizen lawsuits had been responsible before this date for the end of DDT use in many local and state jurisdictions. (Michigan and Arizona, for example, had banned the use of the pesticide in 1968.) Since the banning of DDT, other chlorinated compounds and organophosphates (types of pesticides) have been developed. Many of these compounds are much more toxic than DDT, but lose their toxicity quickly and break down into relatively harmless products. While farmers applied pounds of DDT per acre, only grams per acre of the newer pesticides are required. Moreover, the newer pesticides are often designed to destroy only specific insects or weeds.

Problems continue

Despite these efforts, the effects of the DDT overuse have not been completely erased. In fact, statistics show that toxic compounds may have entered the entire ecosystem of the earth (the complex community of organisms in nature). In *Silent Spring,* Carson predicted the increasing resistance of insects to DDT and other pesticides. This prediction, which was based on scientific evidence available to her at the time—the late 1950s and early 1960s—has proven to be accurate in the years since. Environmental scientists fear that the ecosystem contains toxic compounds that may affect future organisms in unknown ways.

The effects of DDT on humans

The long-term effects of DDT on humans have not been fully determined. Research being carried out worldwide shows that the chemical is found in all human blood and fat, and shows up in high levels in mother's milk in the tropics. There are instances of people being exposed to relatively large amounts of DDT without exhibiting obvious symptoms of poisoning. For example, the small city of Triana, Alabama, is located downstream from the U.S. Army's Redstone Arsenal. The Olin Chemical Company manufactured the pesticide at this site from 1947 until 1970, pouring tons of DDT-laden wastewater into Indian Creek, which runs through Triana. The local fish and water bird population diminished significantly. Triana residents who ate the Indian Creek fish, however, accumulated high levels of DDT and other chlorinated compounds without exhibiting noticeable effects.

Evidence suggests that high DDT levels may affect the behavior of children, increase suicide among older people, and either cause pancreatic cancer or increase the chances of its occurrence. More recently, a study by Mary Wolff of the Mount Sinai School of Medicine in New York City tied DDT levels in women to breast cancer. An increase in breast cancer was known to have coincided with the widespread application of DDT, but this study, published in 1993 by the *Journal of the National Cancer Institute*, is the first to establish a statistical link.

FOR FURTHER REFERENCE

Books

Carson, Rachel. *Silent Spring*. New York City: Houghton Mifflin, 1962.

Periodicals

"The Joy Ride Is Over: Farmers Are Discovering That Pesticides Increasingly Don't Kill Pests." *U.S. News & World Report.* September 14, 1992, pp. 73–74.

Love Canal Toxic Waste Contamination

BEGINNING IN 1942

L ove Canal, near Niagara Falls, New York, is probably the best known—and most infamous—toxic waste site in America. Between 1942 and 1953, Hooker Chemical Corporation buried over 20,000 tons of deadly chemical waste in the small town. By 1980 an entire Love Canal neighborhood built on top of the toxins had to be evacuated after the area was labeled a threat to public health. The community's ordeal was so devastating that the term "Love Canal" came to symbolize chemical contamination of neighborhoods and land areas.

The Love Canal disaster was largely the result of negligence by officials of the Hooker Chemical Corporation. In 1953 the company donated it's contaminated land to the local board of education for a token (symbolic) payment of one dollar. Hooker never clearly warned the buyers about the dangerous nature of the chemicals buried at the site. The company remained silent even when a school, homes, and playgrounds were constructed in the area. Many of the compounds dumped at the site were known to cause cancer, miscarriages, birth defects, and other illnesses and disorders.

Government pressured to take action

By 1976 several years of unusually heavy rains had raised the water table at Love Canal. As basements became flooded, homes

Toxic waste contamination at Love Canal caused so many problems that the term "Love Canal" became a symbol for toxin mismanagement.

In 1980 President Jimmy Carter declared Love Canal a federal disaster area. The total cost for the site's cleanup has been estimated at $250 million.

began to reek of chemicals. Children and pets came home with chemical burns on their feet and hands. Some pets even died, as did trees, flowers, and vegetables. Soon, people in the neighborhood began to experience an extraordinarily high number of serious and unexplainable illnesses, including higher-than-normal rates of cancer, miscarriage, and newborn deformity.

As the number of people experiencing health problems rose, it became increasingly apparent that Love Canal might not be safe for human habitation. Finally pressured by neighborhood activists and negative nationwide publicity, government officials recognized the need for action. In August 1978, New York State health commissioner Dr. Robert P. Whalen recommended that pregnant women and children under the age of two be evacuated from the area. In his report Whalen cited "growing evidence of ... health hazards, as well as spontaneous [unplanned] abortions and congenital [inherited] malformations" at the site. Later that month, the state tested the air,

LOVE CANAL BECOMES HOUSEHOLD NAME In 1978 a twenty-seven-year-old Love Canal housewife named Lois Gibbs became alarmed by the escalating health problems in her community. Frustrated by lack of action on the part of local, state, and federal authorities, she took matters into her own hands. Gibbs organized her neighbors into the Love Canal Homeowners' Association. The group began an over two-year fight to require the government to relocate residents to another area. In the process, Gibbs turned Love Canal into a household name, focusing attention on the growing problem of toxic waste disposal across the country. Her efforts culminated in the passage of the Superfund Law in 1980, which was supposed to generate money for the cleanup of hazardous waste sites. Unfortunately, because of lax government enforcement, the Superfund Law has had minimal effect.

water, soil, and homes for toxic (poisonous) chemicals. Over eighty different compounds were found, and many were thought to be carcinogenic (capable of causing cancer). Chemical pollution of the air was measured at 250 to 5,000 thousand times the levels considered safe.

Studies show alarming effects

The 1978 study found an unusually high miscarriage rate of over twenty-nine percent in the neighborhood, with five of the twenty-four children born in the area listed as having birth defects. State health officials estimated that women in the area had a fifty percent higher than normal risk of miscarriage. Another report found that in 1979, only two of seventeen pregnant women in Love Canal gave birth to normal children. Four others had miscarriages, two had stillbirths (the infants were dead at birth), and nine had babies born with physical defects.

Research conducted by epidemiologists (scientists who study the incidence of disease in a population) revealed an alarming pattern of illness among exposed residents. For example, on Ninety-sixth Street, where fifteen homes were located, eight people developed cancer in the twelve-year period between 1968 and 1980. Six women had cancerous breasts removed, one man contracted bladder cancer, and another man developed throat cancer. In addition, a seven-year-old boy experienced convulsions and died of kidney failure. A pet dog had to be destroyed after developing cancerous tumors.

President declares Love Canal a disaster area

In 1980 further testing revealed high levels of genetic damage among Love Canal residents. An additional 710 families were evacuated at a cost estimated between $3 million and $60 million. That same year, President Jimmy Carter declared the neighborhood a disaster area. In the end, some sixty families decided to remain in their homes, rejecting the government's offer to buy their property. The total cost for the cleanup has been estimated at $250 million. Twelve years after the neighborhood was abandoned, the state of New York approved plans to allow families to move back into some parts of the area, and the sale of homes was permitted.

Hooker downplays disaster

Publicity generated by Love Canal drew national attention to the dangers of toxic chemicals and hazardous waste. Citizens pressured Congress to pass laws to address problems caused by such pollution. Public outrage was particularly fueled by revelations that Hooker Chemical Corporation had covered up the dangers at Love Canal. When Hooker deeded the land to the Niagara Falls Board of Education for one dollar in 1953, the company did not reveal the lethal (deadly) nature of the chemicals it had buried there. Yet Hooker took pains to protect itself: The company drew up a legal agreement that made the school board directly responsible for any deaths, injuries, or lawsuits resulting from exposure to the buried chemicals.

Even when a neighborhood was being built in the area, Hooker failed to issue any warnings. For instance, a 1958 company memo noted that "the entire area is being used as a playground," and that "3 or 4 children had been burned by material at the old Love Canal property." Nevertheless, Hooker remained silent. Ten years later, when a highway was being built near Love Canal, workers uncovered leaking drums full of toxic chemicals.

Industry supports Hooker Chemical

Long after evidence of toxic contamination was uncovered at Love Canal, the chemical industry continued to downplay the

Lois Gibbs organized her neighbors into the Love Canal Homeowners' Association. The association fought for over two years to convince the government to relocate residents to another area.

threats to public health. On October 14, 1979, Armand Hammer discussed Love Canal on the National Broadcasting Corporation (NBC-TV) television program *Meet the Press*. As chairman of Hooker's parent company, Occidental Petroleum Corporation, Hammer said the problem had "been blown up out of context." At Occidental's annual stockholders' meeting the following year, the company rejected a resolution to prevent future Love Canals. The vice president of the Chemical Manufacturers Association, Geraldine Cox, also dismissed the significance of Love Canal. During an interview on the *MacNeil/Lehrer News Hour,* a Public Broadcasting Service (PBS-TV) television show, Cox suggested that Love Canal residents were hypochondriacs (people who have imaginary or exaggerated illnesses).

Waste dumps across America

By 1980 other toxic waste dumps—and potential Love Canals—had been identified. The U.S. Environmental

INVESTIGATOR EXPOSES
PROBLEM Some of the most alarming
Love Canal health data was gathered by Dr.
Beverly Paigen of the Roswell Cancer
Institute. On March 21, 1979, Paigen
testified before the U.S. House
Subcommittee on Oversight and
Investigations. She described the tragic
history of several families directly over or
near liquid wastes that were seeping out of
the ground. In her testimony Paigen
reported a wide range of health problems
such as birth defects, nervous breakdowns,
epilepsy, asthma, bronchitis, urinary disease,
and suicide. Significantly, Paigen observed
that Love Canal residents suffering from
illnesses reported marked health
improvements when they moved out of the
area. Eventually, New York State authorities
declared Love Canal a "grave and imminent
peril" to the health of those living nearby.
Several hundred families were moved out
of the neighborhood, and other residents
were advised to leave. The school was
closed and a barbed wire fence was
placed around it.

Protection Agency (EPA) verified 32,000 to 50,000 thousand hazardous waste disposal sites in the United States. The EPA determined that as many as 1,200 to 2,000 sites might pose "significant risks to human health or the environment." More alarmingly, new chemical waste sites were being discovered at a rate of two hundred a month.

At the time, the EPA estimated that only about 10 percent of the 150 million tons of hazardous wastes generated each year were disposed of in a safe and legal manner. In fact, ninety percent of hazardous wastes posed a potential threat to humans or the environment. The agency called the situation "the most serious environmental problem in the U.S. today." In 1979 U.S. Assistant Attorney General James Moorman testified before the U.S. House Subcommittee on Oversight and Investigations. He announced that toxic waste dumping was the "first or second most serious environmental problem in the country." Moorman also pointed to ineffective environmental regulations and a lack of enforcement of existing anti-dumping laws.

Superfund created

Since the Love Canal disaster, laws designed to protect the public from toxic chemicals have been passed or strengthened. In 1980 a provision of the Resource Conservation and Recovery Act (RCRA) required that toxic wastes be tracked "from cradle to grave." That same year President Carter signed the Superfund Law, which created a fund to pay for the cleanup of hazardous waste sites. According to the law, owners and operators of waste disposal sites, as well as producers and transporters of hazardous materials, are liable (responsible) for cleanup costs. Government enforcement of these measures, however, has been weak. As of the early 1990s, only 149 of 1,256 priority Superfund sites had been cleaned up.

Industry begins taking initiative

Despite lack of government enforcement of environmental regulations, the chemical industry had begun recycling much of its waste by the 1990s. Nevertheless, toxic waste disposal remained a critical problem. In 1993 the Agency for Toxic Substances and Disease Registry estimated that 64,000 areas contaminated by hazardous wastes still required cleanup. Moreover, some forty-one million Americans were living within four miles of a hazardous waste site and might be at some risk. At least two hundred fifty thousand people had been affected by "acute release events," such as toxic waste spills or accidents. Numerous studies show that people living near waste dumps continue to experience birth defects, cancer, and other serious health problems.

It may be impossible to completely clean up the nation's dump sites at any price, but the anticipated costs for the next few years are staggering. One EPA study estimated that it would cost over forty-four billion tax dollars just to clean up the most dangerous sites. Other projections put the figure for addressing Superfund waste sites at more than a trillion dollars over the fifty years.

FOR FURTHER REFERENCE

Books

Gibbs, Lois. *Love Canal: My Story.* Ithaca: State University of New York Press, 1982.

Periodicals

Brown, M. H. "A Toxic Ghost Town: Ten Years Later, Scientists Are Still Assessing the Damage from Love Canal." *Atlantic.* July 1989, pp. 23–26.

Howard Hughes and the *Spruce Goose*

1942 TO 1947

"Well, the airplane seems

to be fairly successful."

—Howard Hughes

Howard Hughes (1905–1976) was a wealthy industrialist who loved airplanes. In fact, Hughes spent most of his life building and flying aircraft. After buying Trans World Airlines (TWA) in 1940, Hughes designed the Lockheed Constellation (also called the "Connie"), a propeller-driven commercial airliner that expanded TWA service around the world. Hughes is also known, however, for building the *Spruce Goose*, a twenty-one-ton military flying boat that has become an American symbol of excess.

According to certain accounts, Hughes was a tragic figure. Some Hughes biographers claim that he suffered from obsessive-compulsive disorder (OCD), a mental illness resulting from a chemical imbalance in the brain. Hughes never seemed to know when to quit working, a fact evidenced by his overwhelming dedication to the TWA/Constellation line and the *Spruce Goose*. He continued building both of these planes even after their design had become obsolete (outdated).

A successful young man

Hughes was born in Houston, Texas. His father, who was the owner of the Hughes Tool Company, had invented a special

Howard Hughes (standing, far right) inspects the engineer's panel of the *Spruce Goose* prior to the plane's test flight. On November 2, 1947, Hughes flew the plane about one mile, then touched down.

device that revolutionized oil drilling. After his father died, Hughes inherited Hughes Tool Company at age nineteen and became an instant millionaire. Hughes was a brilliant mathematician. His natural genius, combined with his immense wealth, enabled the young man to embark on some great adventures that included film making, designing and building airplanes, and flying around the world.

The *Spruce Goose* | 245

THE TWA SUPER-CONSTELLATION CRASH

When millionaire Howard Hughes designed the Lockheed Constellation (also called the "Connie") in 1940, commercial aviation was expanding rapidly. Even though the Connie enabled Trans World Airlines (TWA) to fly all over the globe, the plane was involved in some serious crashes. One of the worst accidents occurred on June 30, 1956, when a TWA Super-Constellation collided with a United Airlines DC-7 in empty airspace over the Grand Canyon in Arizona (see "Science and Technology" entry). All of the 128 passengers aboard the two planes perished. At the time, the crash had the highest single-accident death toll in American history. Even though many aviation experts criticized Hughes for his impractical designs, this particular crash was not necessarily his fault.

The collision of the Constellation and the DC-7 was an example of technology outpacing safety measures. Two of the biggest factors in the accident were an obsolete air traffic control system and limited cockpit visibility. On June 30, the pilots of both planes decided to fly in airspace that was not monitored by air traffic control. Consequently, the pilots were restricted to only what they could see from their cockpit windows. Hughes could be blamed for making these windows too small in the Constellation, but the DC-7 also had limited cockpit visibility. There were simply too many planes in the sky and they were traveling too fast for air traffic controllers to keep up with them. Ironically, the "jet age," when planes would be traveling even faster, was just around the corner.

In 1930 Hughes released *Hell's Angels,* a multi-million-dollar movie that he had produced and directed. The technologically innovative film featured authentic World War I (1914–18) fighter planes in action and realistically portrayed the fiery destruction of a German airship. Later in the decade, Hughes started the Hughes Aircraft Company so that he could build racing planes. On September 13, 1935, Hughes set a world speed record of 352.39 miles per hour in a plane that he designed called the H-1 racer. In 1938 Hughes rebuilt a Lockheed Lodestar airplane. With four crew members, he flew the Lodestar around the world in the record-breaking time of three days, nineteen hours, and fourteen minutes.

Builds the Connie

When Hughes bought TWA in 1940, he wanted to expand the airline's service worldwide. In order to achieve this goal, Hughes needed a propeller-driven airplane with a pressurized cabin (a compartment that maintains normal atmospheric conditions) that could travel high and fast. Thus, the idea for the

Connie was born. Hughes claimed the Connie could fly 300 miles per hour and transport its passengers in unparalleled luxurious comfort. The young man was so confident about his plane that on its maiden (first) voyage he loaded the Connie full of Hollywood celebrities. The plane flew from Los Angeles, California, to Washington, D.C., in a little over six hours.

Although the Connie turned out to be a successful plane, Hughes was unable to start production immediately because no one in the aircraft industry wanted to build it. Everyone thought Hughes was a dreamer, and that a 300-mile-per-hour airplane with a pressurized cabin could not be built. Hughes also wanted the plane to have three vertical (straight up and down) tail fins instead of one. Most designers thought this was an impractical idea, but Hughes insisted that three fins would give the plane a smoother, more stable flight. The inventive aviator would have built the Connie himself, but government regulations did not allow the owner of an airline to build his own planes. Fortunately, the Lockheed Corporation agreed to build the Connie, tail fins and all.

Begins building the Spruce Goose

The story behind the *Spruce Goose* involves more than just Hughes and his love for airplanes. The original idea for a sea plane came from shipbuilder Henry John Kaiser (1882–1967). During World War II (1939–45), German U-boats (a type of submarine) were sinking American cargo ships off beaches on the East Coast of the United States. As a result, the U.S. Army needed a safe way to transport soldiers and supplies to their destinations. Kaiser suggested building an immense cargo ship that could simply fly over the U-boats and their deadly torpedoes. He took his idea to Hughes, who had the technology (and money) to build such a vessel. In 1942 the two men were awarded a contract by the government to build three seaplanes for the army and the *Spruce Goose* project was born.

Problems arise

The seaplane project never went smoothly. A major problem was that the army could not supply the metal necessary to build the plane, so Hughes and Kaiser had to build aircraft out of wood. Originally, the official name of the *Spruce Goose* was the HK-1 (following the initials of Hughes and Kaiser), but Hughes later renamed it the H-4 Hercules when Kaiser left the project because the two men could not get along.

Probably the biggest problem with the *Spruce Goose* project was Hughes's mismanagement. Other high-ranking members of the program complained that Hughes was difficult to locate when they needed him and that he had no respect for authority. For instance, when he wanted something changed, Hughes skipped over the foreman (the on-site man in charge of the job) and delivered orders straight to the workman assigned to a certain task. This led to mass confusion so that it took longer than the allotted two years to build the *Spruce Goose*.

Finishes *Spruce Goose*

In 1944—after the allotted time of two years—the government canceled the seaplane program. By 1945 World War II ended, so the plane was no longer needed. Despite the fact that the *Spruce Goose* would never be used for its intended purpose, Hughes finished building the craft anyway. When Hughes was finally finished with the plane, he had spent $22 million of the government's money and $7 million of his own. Despite these huge expenditures, rumors were spreading throughout the government and the aviation industry that the costly project was a complete failure. Critics believed the *Spruce Goose* would never fly. This infuriated Hughes, making him even more determined to fly the plane.

The *Spruce Goose* was huge. It was three times larger than any plane ever built. Measuring 220 feet in length, it had a tail that stood almost ten stories high. The wings, which spanned 340 feet, were so thick that flight engineers could walk around inside of them. The plane had three hydraulic systems and an electrical system with triple-redundancy (a multiple backup system). The immense propeller-driven airplane was powered by eight three-thousand-horsepower Pratt-Whitney R-4360 radial engines with twenty-eight cylinders each. With a total of 24,000 horsepower, The *Spruce Goose* had a top speed of 200 miles per hour and— with 14 fuel tanks holding 1,000 gallons each—a range of 3,500 miles. The *Spruce Goose* was able to carry 700 fully equipped soldiers and an entire medical staff safely across the ocean.

The *Spruce Goose* was a very large aircraft. It measured over 200 feet in length and had a wingspan of 340 feet.

Spruce Goose flies

Before Hughes could fly the *Spruce Goose,* however, he had to move it. In June 1946 he paid $60,000 to have the plane moved twenty-eight miles from its hangar in Culver City, California, to Long Beach, California. More than 2,000 people were involved in the move, which took five days. Trees had to be trimmed, traffic had to be rerouted, and utility wires had to be temporarily dismantled to make way for the enormous boat plane. It was such a big event that schools were dismissed along the route so that students could watch the great wooden plane pass by. Finally, on November 2, 1947, Hughes decided to fly the *Spruce Goose.* At first he had planned to just taxi up and down the harbor, but the engines performed so well that he decided to take off. Hughes lifted the seaplane only about seventy feet above the water, flew it about a mile, then touched down. The historic flight lasted only about ninety seconds. It was the first and last time the *Spruce Goose* ever flew.

Loses TWA

Three years after Hughes flew the *Spruce Goose,* a new era in aviation technology was born. The jet age of the 1950s heralded jet-powered planes that could fly higher and faster than the old propeller-driven airplanes. In the wake of this new technology, the Hughes empire crashed. The Constellation line and the *Spruce Goose* were fine examples of classic propeller-driven airplanes, but they were no match for the new jet-powered airliners. The jet age delivered a powerful blow to Hughes. He lost TWA, then began to suffer the first of many long-term ailments.

When Hughes built the Connie in 1940, the aviation industry was impressed with the natural abilities of the pioneering industrialist. Ten years later, however, these same industry officials were asking themselves why Hughes would not adapt to the changing times. By 1956, TWA's major rivals had all purchased new jetliners such as the Boeing 707 or the Douglas Aircraft DC-8. TWA, on the other hand, was stuck with the reliable, but comparatively slow, Constellation. For some reason, Hughes refused to buy a new fleet of jets for his airline until it was too late. In 1960, TWA sued Hughes for mismanagement, claiming the corporation had lost $438 million in business from 1958 to 1959. TWA officials complained that it had taken Hughes too long to buy new jets for the company, and that in the meantime they had lost their competitive edge. Hughes responded in 1966 by selling all his TWA stock for $568 million, which at the time was the largest sum ever acquired in a business deal by a single individual.

Health declines

Between 1966 and 1968, Hughes took the money he had earned from the TWA deal and bought several casinos and hotels in Las Vegas, Nevada. As a result, Hughes eventually became a billionaire. Now suffering intensely from OCD, Hughes was completely isolated from the people who had once been close to him. He was also in an almost constant disoriented (confused) state due to the severe head injuries he had sustained in the crash of an XF-11 spy plane in 1946. Unable to care for himself, the eccentric billionaire let his hair and fingernails grow long. Eventually becoming a recluse (a person who shuns contact with other people), Hughes spent the rest of his life in squalor under the control of a group of unethical advisors.

SCHEMERS SEEK PROFIT FROM HUGHES'S NAME

Because Howard Hughes was a billionaire, he was often surrounded by greedy people who wanted a share of his fortune. Some of these people used scams, or hoaxes, to make money off of Hughes. For example, on December 7, 1971, *The Memoirs of Howard Hughes: His True Life Story as Told to Clifford Irving* was released. The author, Clifford Irving, was a moderately successful writer who claimed he had spent two years interviewing Hughes for the book. Hughes responded on January 7, 1972, by announcing publicly that he had never heard of Irving. The author later confessed to the hoax and served time in prison.

Another apparent hoax took place in the 1970s when a will that had allegedly been handwritten by Hughes turned up at the Mormon church headquarters in Salt Lake City, Utah. The document stated that Melvin Dummar, a gas station owner from Utah, should inherit one-sixteenth of the Hughes estate. Dummar claimed to have actually met the billionaire before he died. No charges were pressed when the will was dismissed as a fake. Dummar played a cameo role in *Melvin and Howard* (1980), a film about the incident that featured actor Jason Robards as Hughes.

Hughes legacy lives on

Despite Hughes's rather tragic fate, his legacy lives on. Even though the eccentric billionaire encountered significant misfortune throughout his life, he also made successful and enduring contributions to society. For instance, one of America's largest sponsors of medical research, the Howard Hughes Medical Institute, still exists today. The *Spruce Goose* also survived intact. It was moved on August 10, 1992, and now resides in a hangar in McMinnville, Oregon. Hughes's best films—*Hell's Angels, Scarface* (1922), and *The Outlaw* (1943)— are testaments to the fact that Hughes was an accomplished producer and director.

In addition to the Constellation and the *Spruce Goose*, Hughes made other substantial breakthroughs in the field of aviation; he also invented many useful weapons for the military. For his record-breaking flights, he received the prestigious Harmon International Trophy from President Franklin D. Roosevelt in 1937. As the founder of Hughes Aircraft in 1932, Hughes is credited with the invention of retractable landing gear (gear that draw up into the body of a plane) and an oxygen feeder system for pilots. After starting Hughes Electronics in 1940, he invented several military weapons, including a seek-and-find radar system and the revolutionary air-to-air combat missile that is still in use. Hughes also pioneered unmanned satellite prototypes (models) that paved the way for contemporary satellite programs. In recognition for his many achievements, Hughes was inducted into the Aviation Hall of Fame in Dayton, Ohio, on December 14, 1973.

FOR FURTHER READING

Books

Barton, Charles. *Howard Hughes and His Flying Boat.* Fallbrook, CA: Aero Publishers, 1982.

Thalidomide Birth Defects

LATE 1950S TO EARLY 1960S

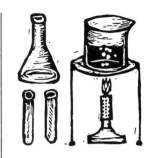

Thalidomide caused birth defects in thousands of babies whose mothers had taken the drug during pregnancy.

In the early 1960s, the over-the-counter pharmaceutical (nonprescription drug) Thalidomide was marketed as a sedative (sleep aid) and antinausea drug in more than forty countries. (Nausea is a feeling of sickness in the stomach characterized by the need to vomit. It is a common side effect of morning sickness.) Within six years the drug was found to cause birth defects in thousands of babies whose mothers had taken the drug to prevent morning sickness during pregnancy. Many "Thalidomide children" were born without arms or legs. Others were blind and deaf or had heart defects or intestinal abnormalities. In some cases, the infants' birth defects were even more severe, with some children being born without eyes or ears.

While some Thalidomide babies were mentally retarded, most were of normal intelligence. It is thought that all together more than 10,000 babies around the world were affected by Thalidomide. This horrible tragedy led directly to a strengthening of the laws regulating the development and sale of prescription and nonprescription drugs on four continents and to vastly improved testing of new drugs in the United States.

Trial and error

Historically, new pharmaceuticals were developed by trial and error. Organic chemists (scientists who study chemical reactions in the body) first synthesized (combined) new chemical compounds. The compounds were next evaluated by pharmacologists (scientists who study the effects of drugs) for beneficial effects on lab animals. If a compound was found to have a desirable effect in the animals, the study was expanded to human volunteers and finally to the general public. Even when performed correctly by scientists under favorable conditions, however, the testing procedure did not always result in the development of safe and effective drugs. Sometimes, incompetent scientists or greedy executives rushed a new drug to market, with disastrous results. This is what happened in the case of Thalidomide.

A money-making product

Thalidomide was originally developed in 1954 by Chemie Grünenthal, a West German pharmaceuticals company. At the time, Grünenthal made most of its money by marketing, under license, pharmaceuticals developed in other countries. Profit margins for marketing other companies' pharmaceuticals, however, were generally low. Grünenthal's scientists (many of whom had no formal training in pharmacology) were under great pressure to develop new drugs for the West German market. These "in-house" drugs could be sold without Chemie Grünenthal having to pay royalties.

Little testing done

Due to Thalidomide's projected high profit margin, Grünenthal rushed the drug to market. Before its release, however, Thalidomide was only tested in limited animal studies and superficial clinical trials on human beings. None of these tests were verified by other laboratories, and none were done using standard double-blind testing. (In double-blind testing, neither the doctor nor the patient knows if the patient is receiving the drug or a harmless placebo, a substance that will produce no effects).

By May 1961 Thalidomide was the most successful product in the history of the Grünenthal corporation. It accounted for more than half of the company's revenues and was by far the most popular over-the-counter sedative on the market in West Germany. Thalidomide was marketed as a cure for everything from the flu to morning sickness. The greatest selling point was

POSSIBLE TREATMENT FOR AIDS One side effect of Thalidomide is the inhibition (or repression) of tumor necrosis factor (TNF). Scientists have found that this may prove useful in the treatment of AIDS (acquired immunodeficiency syndrome), a breakdown of the body's immune system. A natural substance that normally defends the body against cancer and infections, TNF promotes the production of the human immunodeficiency virus (HIV). Some AIDS patients who have taken Thalidomide have gained weight and no longer experience fevers. Although researchers do not consider Thalidomide a potential cure for AIDS, they believe the drug may prove effective in slowing the progress of the disease by suppressing the production of HIV in infected cells. In 1997 the U.S. Food and Drug Administration approved the use of Thalidomide in the treatment of AIDS.

Thalidomide's safety: Grünenthal claimed the drug was completely nontoxic (nonpoisonous) and had no side effects.

The success of Thalidomide in West Germany did not escape the notice of pharmaceutical companies throughout the rest of the world. Licenses to manufacture the drug were obtained by pharmaceutical companies in Britain, Japan, France, Italy, Australia, and the world's largest market for over-the-counter remedies, the United States.

Relationship to birth defects discovered

Thalidomide had been on the market for more than six years and had caused birth defects in nearly four thousand babies—mostly in West Germany—before anyone began to suspect that the drug might be dangerous. Thalidomide was first identified as the cause of birth defects by William McBride, an Australian obstetrician. McBride had delivered three babies in the first six months of 1961 with nearly identical birth defects: no radius bone (the shorter of the two bones in the forearm) in either arm and bowel atresia (the lower intestine has no opening to the anus). All three babies died shortly after birth.

McBride researched medical literature for information on birth defects, especially bowel atresias. What he read led him to believe that the abnormalities he had seen in his practice were caused by an adverse drug reaction. Upon examining the hospital records of the three women who had given birth to the malformed babies, he found that all of them had been given

Thalidomide during their pregnancies. (It was also the only drug any of the women had taken during their pregnancies.) For McBride, this seemed to be compelling evidence that Thalidomide was the cause of the birth defects and that it should be withdrawn from use until further studies could be conducted.

Doctor writes paper

McBride immediately notified the local distributor of Thalidomide that the drug was causing birth defects. He then submitted a paper to *The Lancet,* one of the world's most prestigious medical journals, detailing his theory about Thalidomide. McBride was ignored by the drug companies, and *The Lancet* refused to publish his paper. More than six months later the medical establishment admitted that McBride had been right. In the meantime, thousands more babies had died and even more infants had been born with deformities.

FDA intervenes

Except for the courage of a single doctor working for the United States Food and Drug Administration (FDA), the Thalidomide disaster could have been far worse than it actually was. Shortly before McBride delivered his first Thalidomide baby, Richardson-Merrel, makers of Vicks VapoRub, submitted an application to the FDA to market Thalidomide over the counter in the United States. Richardson-Merrel had big plans for the drug. In fact, the company had already distributed more than two million Thalidomide pills to more than twelve hundred doctors. In turn, the doctors had administered the drug to approximately twenty thousand patients. All of this took place even before Richardson-Merrel had submitted its application for FDA approval of Thalidomide for use in human beings.

Throughout 1961, Frances Oldham Kelsey, a medical officer at the FDA, rejected Richardson-Merrel's application on six different occasions. Kelsey almost singlehandedly faced down the huge company, which exerted strong pressure on the doctor and her superiors to approve Thalidomide for use in the United States. After threatening Kelsey with a libel suit (a suit that claims one party has damaged another party in a written statement), Richardson-Merrel withdrew its application (but only after Thalidomide had been withdrawn from the market in West Germany). For her courage, President John F. Kennedy awarded Kelsey the Distinguished Federal Civilian Service Medal, the highest award given to civilians in government service.

After the Thalidomide disaster, the Food, Drug and Cosmetics Act of 1938 (which the FDA is charged with enforcing) was modified by the passage of the Kefauver-Harris Act of 1962. The Kefauver-Harris Act greatly strengthened the FDA by requiring that pharmaceutical companies prove drugs to be both safe and effective (prior to Thalidomide, pharmaceutical companies only had to show a drug was safe). The act also widely expanded the FDA's powers to regulate the development and testing of new drugs.

Drug-testing regulations strengthened

After Thalidomide, pharmaceutical companies were required to show that the doctors testing new drugs were qualified and that the tests being conducted were safe, controlled, and verifiable. In addition, no person was given a drug without being informed that the drug was experimental. Companies were required to report all of the results of all of their tests, not just those trials that showed their new drugs in a favorable light.

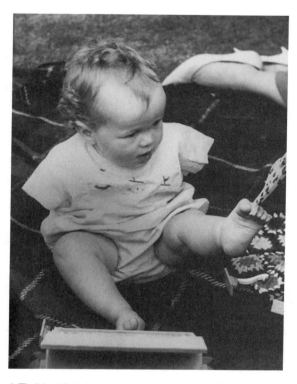

A Thalidomide baby at sixteen months of age. Many Thalidomide children were born without arms or legs. Others were blind and deaf, or had heart defects or intestinal abnormalities.

All drug trials in the United States were also required to study the effects of a drug on human fetuses (human embryos in the later stages of development). In the case of Thalidomide, the drug did not lead to deformities in rat fetuses, but it did produce nearly identical deformities to those found in human beings in rabbit fetuses. For this reason, every new drug tested in the United States is tested in multiple animal species prior to its study in human beings.

In the wake of the Thalidomide tragedy, conflict-of-interest rules were passed forbidding FDA employees from accepting money from pharmaceutical companies. Perhaps the most far-reaching result of the Thalidomide disaster was the example set by Kelsey. Her moral courage under extreme pressure set a standard of conduct for other FDA doctors and scientists.

FOR FURTHER REFERENCE

Books

Knightley, P., H. Evans, E. Potter, and M. Wallace. *Suffer the Children: The Story of Thalidomide*. New York City: Viking Press, 1979.

Periodicals

Stolberg, Sheryl Gay. "Thalidomide Gets U.S. Approval to Aid Lepers and Maybe Others." *The New York Times*. July 17, 1998, pp. A1, A14.

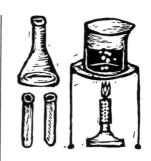

TWA Super-Constellation and United Airlines DC-7 Collision

JUNE 30, 1956

At the time, the crash created the highest single-accident death toll in the history of commercial aviation.

On June 30, 1956, two propeller-driven commercial airliners, a TWA Super-Constellation (sometimes called a "Connie") and a United Airlines DC-7, collided in empty airspace over the Grand Canyon in Arizona. There were 128 people aboard the two planes—all the passengers and crew perished. At the time, the crash created the highest single-accident death toll in the history of commercial aviation. During a series of post-crash investigations, the accident revealed that flight technology was outpacing safety. The condition of the Civil Aeronautics Administration (CAA) air traffic control system in 1956 was very poor. Not only was the system outdated, but airplanes—especially jet airliners— were traveling too fast to be safely tracked. In August 1958 Congress passed the Federal Aviation Act, which President Dwight D.Eisenhower quickly signed into law. The act established an independent Federal Aviation Administration (FAA), which had almost total jurisdiction over civil and military air traffic. This new agency had authority and funding to modernize air traffic control and drastically expand controlled airspace.

A fatal coincidence

The midair collision of the TWA Super-Constellation and the United Airlines DC-7 occurred because the planes' crews

CONNIE DESIGNED BY HOWARD HUGHES One of the airplanes involved in the 1956 collision over the Grand Canyon was a Lockheed Constellation designed by wealthy industrialist Howard Hughes. After buying Trans World Airlines (TWA) in 1940, Hughes designed the Constellation as the company's new flagship airliner. At first, experts objected to the Constellation's triple-tail design, even though Hughes insisted it would help the plane fly better. Even though the Constellation—and its unusual design—turned out to be a success, it was soon eclipsed by faster, sleeker jetliners. When Hughes refused to buy new jets, TWA sued him for mismanagement, claiming the company had lost $438 million in business. Hughes responded by selling his TWA stock.

were given similar flight plans by Air Route Traffic Control (ARTC). The planes had left Los Angeles, California, within minutes of each other, and both were heading east. Both planes were flying off airways—that is, using airspace uncontrolled by ARTC centers. The captain of each airplane had chosen his route either because the controlled airways were too clogged or the "off airways" flight plan was more direct.

The captains' decision to fly on uncontrolled routes was not unusual. At that time the ARTC lacked sufficient personnel and proper facilities to completely monitor all airspace. The flight plans of the Constellation and the DC-7 therefore specified that their crews would be operating under "visual flight rules" (VFR). This meant they would assume responsibility for avoiding other traffic. A major hazard of VFR, however, was that the pilots were restricted only to what they could see out of the cockpit windows.

Lapse in communication

The crash was set in motion when the Constellation had to change altitudes. Originally, the TWA captain had filed a flight plan that put his plane at a lower altitude than the United Airlines plane. After the TWA captain had brought the Constellation to its assigned cruising altitude, however, it flew into clouds where there was no visibility. As a result, ARTC gave the captain permission to go 1,000 feet higher. This put the Constellation at a cruising altitude of 21,000 feet. The good news was that the TWA plane was now above cloud cover—the

Rescue party members sift through the wreckage of the TWA Super-Constellation and United Airlines DC-7 collision.

bad news was that it was also at the same altitude as the United Airlines DC-7.

An ARTC center immediately alerted the TWA captain that the United Airlines DC-7 was also at 21,000 feet. Understaffed ARTC centers along the route failed to warn the United Airlines captain, however, that the TWA flight had been cleared to the same altitude. One controller later admitted he had noticed that both flights had an identical estimated arrival time over a checkpoint near the Grand Canyon, but he was so preoccupied with handling traffic in his own area that he gave the fatal coincidence no further thought.

An "impossible accident"

The two airplanes, each traveling at approximately 300 miles per hour, collided at an estimated angle of 35 degrees. After the accident, search parties hunted through the wreckage for clues about the crash. First they found one of the

EARLY AIR TRAFFIC CONTROL In the earliest days of commercial aviation, there were no government-run air traffic control procedures. Instead, all of the nation's airlines operated their own traffic control systems. This was a relatively simple task because, as late as 1932, the entire American airline industry consisted of twenty-four carriers. Altogether these carriers operated fewer than 700 daily flights with a fleet of only 450 airplanes.

Eighty percent of these flights were made by small, single-engine aircraft. In recent years, air traffic control has evolved to the point where pilots have their own radar screen in the cockpit. Called "TCAS," this system was deployed in 1988 to avoid midair collisions. All commercial airliners in the United States are required to have TCAS, and most planes in other countries also use the system. The United States military, however, has not yet fully adopted TCAS.

Constellation's three tails. Red, white, and blue paint marks on it had obviously come from a DC-7 propeller. Then they found a rear cargo door from the TWA plane that also had red, white, and blue gouges on it. Civil Aeronautics Board (CAB) investigators concluded that the DC-7 had hit the Constellation. Because the collision occurred in wide-open airspace and in relatively clear weather, investigators determined the crash had been an "impossible accident."

CAA outdated

In fact, it was an accident just waiting to happen. The CAB's final report steered clear of putting the majority of blame on the two flight crews. Instead, the board placed ultimate responsibility on the CAA, the U.S. Department of Commerce, and the U.S. Congress. All of these agencies had allowed aviation technology to outpace an obsolete, overworked air traffic control system.

At the time of the crash, the government-run CAA had replaced systems that had been privately operated by the airlines. In fact, the government had already been controlling the skies for twenty years, but by 1956 procedures and facilities had become obsolete. The CAA was a small, low-priority agency that received all of its funding from the Department of Commerce. When air traffic began booming after World War II (1939–45), several air safety experts warned that traffic control procedures were hopelessly antiquated and potentially dangerous. As one official commented, "We're tracking 300-mile-an-hour airplanes with radar designed to track 20-knot battleships."

Pressure for change

The CAB's final report on the collision merely referred to the system's inadequacies without pinpointing why they existed. This was not necessary, however, because the airlines, air safety experts, lawmakers, the White House, and media were in unanimous agreement on the real reason for the Grand Canyon tragedy—the CAA was not getting enough money. Yet, while Congress debated solutions to the problem, two more midair collisions occurred: a United Airlines DC-7 ran into an Air Force fighter over Las Vegas, Nevada, and a Capital Viscount hit a National Guard fighter near Brunswick, Maryland.

Both military planes were operating under VFR, and the accidents exposed another ARTC weakness—the danger of mixing VFR and controlled traffic, especially when the VFR flights involved swift military planes. The need for improved systems was made even more crucial because, at the time of the Grand Canyon collision, airlines in America were only two years away from inaugurating jet service.

FAA established

In August 1958 Congress finally passed the Federal Aviation Act, which President Dwight D. Eisenhower quickly signed it into law. The act established an independent Federal Aviation Administration (FAA), which had almost total jurisdiction over civil and military air traffic. This new agency had authority and funding to modernize air traffic control and drastically expand controlled airspace.

Ironically, this fully independent agency with its own budget and virtually unlimited powers was tossed aside only eight years later. In 1966 Congress placed the FAA under auspices of the new Department of Transportation. Not only did this relegate the FAA to the same subordinate status as the old CAA, but in the opinion of most aviation observers, it also cost the agency much of its effectiveness.

FOR FURTHER REFERENCE

Periodicals

"Apparent United-TWA Collision Highlights Traffic-Control Problem." *Aviation Weekly.* July 9, 1956, pp. 39–40.

"Perilous Searching Operation: Grand Canyon Crash." *Life.* July 16, 1956, pp. 19–25.

The Chevrolet Corvair Controversy

1959 TO 1963

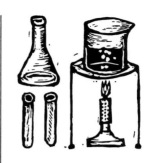

The Chevrolet Corvair was introduced in September 1959 as the first rear-engine automobile mass-produced in the United States. After being put on the market, however, Corvairs were involved in a series of accidents, many of which were fatal. Critics blamed design flaws in the car's fully independent suspension system. (In this suspension system, each wheel can move without affecting the movement of the other wheels.) In addition, the Corvair's direct-air heating system was criticized for drawing strong, potentially dangerous fumes into the passenger compartment. As a result of these design problems, many ground-breaking lawsuits were brought against General Motors, the automobile's manufacturer.

The controversy surrounding the Corvair was heightened by consumer advocate Ralph Nader (1934–), who wrote the book *Unsafe at Any Speed* about problems in the automobile industry. In 1966—in part because of the publicity surrounding the Corvair—the U.S. Congress passed the National Traffic and Motor Vehicle Safety Act. The Safety Act was the first federal legislation to establish government standards for automotive design safety.

As a result of traffic fatalities involving the Chevrolet Corvair, the U.S. Congress passed the National Traffic and Motor Vehicle Safety Act.

A 1960 Chevrolet Corvair. The Corvair's design was quite radical by American automotive industry standards. Not only was the vehicle smaller than the norm, but it also had a rear-mounted engine.

A radical design

The design of the Corvair, a compact car, was quite radical by American automotive industry standards. Not only was the vehicle smaller than the typical American automobile, but it also had a rear-mounted engine like that of the Volkswagen, which was made in Germany. (Until that time, American car engines were mounted in the front of the vehicle.) Another difference was that, like the Volkswagen, the Corvair engine was air cooled. (On American cars the engine had traditionally been cooled by a radiator filled with water and located in front of the engine.) Unlike its imported rival, however, the Corvair featured an innovative transaxle system (a system which joins the transmission, the device that changes gears, with the rear axle).

The design of the Corvair became controversial even before it was introduced to the public. Since a rear-engine car had never been mass-produced in America, many skeptics questioned whether the vehicle could be operated safely. Both the Ford and Chrysler motor companies tried to raise doubts about the Corvair in advance advertisements for their own cars, the Falcon and the Valiant. Magazine reviews of the Corvair, although positive in tone, also raised issues about its high-speed handling.

Car handles poorly

A major concern was that over sixty percent of the Corvair's weight was concentrated on the rear axle, thus making the vehicle potentially hard to handle. Most cars are designed to "understeer," so that their tendency in a high-speed turn is to go straight. This requires the driver to increase the use of the steering wheel in making turns. An "oversteering" car, on the other hand, has a tendency to turn without the assistance of the steering wheel. The driver must therefore concentrate on guiding the car straight during a high-speed turn. Like most cars, the Corvair would understeer at

Consumer advocate Ralph Nader campaigned for automotive industry reform in his book *Unsafe at Any Speed*.

normal speeds. Critics charged, however, that during a high-speed turn, the vehicle would begin to oversteer and go sideways. This phenomenon could get an unskilled and unprepared driver into trouble. The dispute was not over whether the Corvair tended to oversteer—even its defenders did not deny this fact. Instead, the question was when the oversteering would occur, and whether the average driver could be expected to cope with it.

One strategy Corvair designers used to offset the oversteering problem was to require different air pressures for front and rear tires. Although these instructions were spelled out in the owner's manual, they were routinely ignored. Corvair owners who sought advice on the subject at service stations often received incorrect and contradictory information. The failure to maintain the different air pressures increased the tendency of the car to oversteer.

Car rolls over

The other charge against the Corvair related to the design of its rear axle. Nader and other critics claimed that during sharp cornering, the rear wheel could shift by as much as eleven degrees. This shift could cause excessive body sway, greatly increasing the likelihood that the car would roll over. Critics made much of the fact that General Motors had originally included a front anti-roll bar in the Corvair design, but had eliminated it to reduce costs. General Motors fervently denied this allegation, which was never proven. There is, however, some evidence that a handling problem existed. Shortly after the introduction of the Corvair, General Motors began marketing accessories that would improve the car's ride and handling. The best-selling item was the EMPI Camber Compensator, which was widely touted as a cure for the car's suspension ills.

Car has heater problems

Separate allegations about a defective heating system dogged the Corvair from the start. In most automobiles the passenger compartment heater relies on heat drawn from the engine coolant. The Corvair's engine was air-cooled, however, making this approach impossible. The engine's rear location also created complications. The Corvair relied on a system of ducts and an electric fan to route some of the air used to cool the engine into the passenger compartment. If fumes such as oil smoke or carbon monoxide escaped because of worn engine seals, those fumes were pulled into the passenger compartment.

The first fatality

In spite of negative publicity about possible design flaws, the Corvair initially enjoyed respectable sales. In 1960 *Motor Trend* magazine named the auto "Car of the Year"—a coveted honor. Nonetheless, problems began immediately. The first documented Corvair fatality involving a loss of control occurred in 1960, the year the car was released. A California teenager named Don Lyford lost control of his Corvair when making an S-turn and was killed in a collision with an oncoming car. A Los Angeles attorney investigating the accident inter-

THE NATIONAL TRAFFIC AND MOTOR VEHICLE SAFETY ACT The negative publicity surrounding the Corvair resulted in a new attitude toward product safety and manufacturer responsibility. The National Traffic and Motor Vehicle Safety Act developed by Senator Abraham Ribicoff's subcommittee was written primarily by consumer advocate Ralph Nader. Nader regarded auto manufacturers as nothing less than criminals. In Nader's opinion the Safety Act was not nearly strong enough. (For example, he felt that executives should be imprisoned if they did not comply with the law.) Nevertheless, the act created the National Traffic Safety Agency (later called the National Highway Traffic Safety Administration), which drafts the regulations adhered to by all auto manufacturers today.

viewed a police officer who claimed to have seen "six of them [Corvairs] flip out of control" in recent months.

Over the next several years, the same attorney handled numerous lawsuits involving the Corvair against General Motors. None of these cases reached a definite conclusion until 1964. A motorist named Rose Pierini, who had lost an arm in a rollover crash in her Corvair, was awarded seventy thousand dollars in an out-of-court settlement. Widely reported in the press as a victory for Pierini, the settlement opened the floodgate to suits against General Motors.

"The book that killed the Corvair"

In 1965 Nader published a book that escalated the controversy. While only the first chapter of *Unsafe at Any Speed* discussed the Corvair, Nader intended the book to be an indictment of all the Detroit automakers (though his main target was General Motors). The first sentence of Nader's preface reads: "For over half a century, the automobile has brought death, injury, and the most inestimable sorrow and deprivation to millions of people." Nader contended that General Motors executives had marketed the Corvair even when they knew it was unsafe. The company's desire for profit, he said, outweighed all other considerations. In short, Nader essentially accused General Motors of negligent homicide (death caused by indifference to existing problems or situations).

Under ordinary circumstances, *Unsafe at Any Speed* probably would have attracted little notice. But at the time of its publication Nader was on the staff of Senator Abraham Ribicoff, head of a Senate subcommittee that was working on a bill to establish federal standards for automobile design. The book received immediate national attention. During congressional hearings Nader testified as an expert witness on various automotive topics. Contending that the Corvair was unsafe, he recommended the recall of models produced from 1960 to 1963.

Nader's testimony, along with some well-timed publicity, set the stage for strong legislation. In 1966 the National Traffic and Motor Vehicle Safety Act was unanimously passed by both houses of Congress and signed into law by President Lyndon B. Johnson. Nader's role in the passage of the bill established him as spokesman for the new "consumerism." Nevertheless, the congressional hearings did not lead to the recall of all 1960 to 1963 Corvairs, as Nader had demanded. In fact, in spite of Nader's nearly ten years of effort, such measures never took place.

Corvair finally discontinued

In the 1964 Corvair model year, General Motors adopted suspension modifications similar to the Camber Compensator, the device that was marketed to correct handling problems. From that year onward, the incidence of accident-related lawsuits decreased dramatically. The following year, the Corvair's rear suspension was completely redesigned. By that time, however, negative publicity about the car had done its damage. Sales had revived slightly in 1965, but in 1966, the year of the Ribicoff hearings, sales dropped catastrophically—from 209,152 to 88,951 cars. Virtually no design changes occurred in the Corvair between 1966 and 1969. General Motors officially canceled the automobile on May 14, 1969. In that year, only 3,102 Corvairs were produced.

Problems continue

General Motors' litigation problems were not over. Public attention now turned to alleged design flaws in the Corvair's direct-air heater. Throughout the 1960s, the company had received hundreds of letters complaining of acrid fumes coming through heater vents in the Corvair. The fumes not only

A NEW ATTITUDE ABOUT PRODUCT SAFETY The

controversy that began in 1959 with the introduction of the Corvair gave rise to a new legal concept: the liability of an automobile manufacturer for negligence of design safety. Until that time, the view had been that automobile drivers should look out for their own well-being and were responsible for avoiding accidents. Little or no thought was given to designing automobiles so that accidents would be survivable or less injurious. Vehicle interiors, for example, had no seat belts or interior padding, headrests, or knee bolsters. Protruding knobs and horn buttons often produced injuries that, in hindsight, seemed highly preventable. The same was true of protruding fins and hood ornaments on the exterior. Brake systems were not fail-safe, steering columns sometimes broke loose and impaled drivers, and broken windshields became jagged and deadly.

had a strong odor, but they could also be dangerous to passengers. Under continual pressure from consumer advocate groups, the National Highway Traffic Safety Administration finally determined that the Corvair's direct-air heating system "creates an unreasonable risk of accidents and injury to persons." The engine fumes, the agency found, sometimes contained carbon monoxide "in sufficient concentrations to harm or endanger the occupants of the vehicle."

General Motors grudgingly accepted this finding. In December 1971, the corporation mailed a letter to all known Corvair owners suggesting that they take their cars to a dealership for an inspection of the heating system. Since the release of fumes depended on the condition of seals in the engine and heater ducts, General Motors treated the entire issue as a maintenance matter. The company refused to accept any financial responsibility, even for recommended inspections. In the letter General Motors also suggested that winter drivers turn the heater off or roll the windows down if the fumes became too heavy. This advice was not well received by Corvair owners. General Motors, which was already swamped with complaints about suspension flaws, decided to wait out this new tempest. Therefore the company dealt with heater problems one at a time as the Corvairs aged and were removed from service.

In 1972, three years after the Corvair was discontinued, General Motors won a victory in the steering-and-handling controversy. The National Highway Traffic Safety Administration finally issued a report declaring that there was nothing exceptionally wrong with the Corvair's steering design. "The handling and stability performance of the 1960 to 1963 Corvair does not result in an abnormal potential for loss of control or rollover," the agency declared, "and it is at least as good as the performance of some contemporary vehicles both foreign and domestic."

FOR FURTHER REFERENCE

Boooks

Nader, Ralph. *Unsafe at Any Speed.* New York City: Grossman, 1965.

Agent Orange Spraying

1961 TO 1971

During the Vietnam War (1954–75), the United States military used Agent Orange to clear jungles and forests in order to combat Viet Cong guerrillas (soldiers who use unconventional fighting strategies that include ambush). One of the most effective modern herbicides (substances that kill plants or prevent plant growth), Agent Orange is also one of the most toxic (poisonous) because it contains dioxin. Nevertheless, in violation of U.S. government policy, Agent Orange was sprayed indiscriminately during the Vietnam conflict. At the time, however, chemical manufacturers did not disclose to either the government or the public that the defoliant (a chemical applied to plants in order to cause the leaves to drop off prematurely) contained dioxin. Consequently, Vietnam civilians and American soldiers were heavily exposed to dangerously high levels of Agent Orange, which contaminated food and water supplies.

Since the war, Vietnam veterans have charged that they are suffering from cancers and other diseases directly linked to the use of the herbicide. Over the years, however, the chemical companies and the U.S. government have vigorously fought the veterans' claims. As a result, the story behind the use of Agent Orange—and its potential for harm—did not really begin to unfold until the 1990s, more than twenty years after the U.S. military withdrew from Vietnam.

Vietnam veterans have charged that they are suffering from cancers and other diseases directly linked to the use of the Agent Orange.

An effective defoliant

Agent Orange is composed of two herbicides—2,4-D and 2,4,5-T—which are combined in equal amounts to make a highly toxic mixture. The defoliant was used commercially in forestry control as early as the 1930s. Toward the end of World War II (1939–45), the U.S. government considered using Agent Orange during battles in the Pacific. In 1959 the military initiated the first large-scale use of the herbicide when airplanes sprayed it on about four square miles of vegetation at Fort Detrick, Maryland. After the successful experiment, military leaders concluded they had discovered an effective defoliation method.

Requested by South Vietnamese

By 1960 the South Vietnamese government, which was at war with the Communist regime in North Vietnam, had become aware of the American herbicide experiments. (Communism is a political doctrine based on ownership of property by the state. Communists advocate a classless society with an equal distribution of economic goods.) Since the United States was now an ally, South Vietnamese officials suggested testing defoliants as a defense against Viet Cong (Communist North Vietnamese) guerilla forces in the jungles. Although U.S. President John F. Kennedy (1917–1963) supported use of the chemicals, he cautioned that the spraying should be carefully and selectively controlled. (Kennedy was especially concerned about possible contamination of food supplies.) U.S. Secretary of State Dean Rusk warned that Communist and neutral countries (countries not directly involved in the conflict) might accuse the United States of engaging in "germ warfare" (the use of chemical weapons, which is against international law).

Project Ranch Hand

Military leaders strongly favored using defoliants. American soldiers were not accustomed to fighting in jungle conditions, they argued, so it was necessary to clear the heavy vegetation. Otherwise, communication would be impossible and

◀ Three United States Air Force planes spray Agent Orange over a jungle area in South Vietnam.

soldiers could not carry out battle strategies. A defoliant-spraying program was finally approved. In the early stages of the war fifteen varieties of chemicals were used as herbicides. The colors they produced—blue, purple, orange, pink, and green—were called the "rainbow of destruction."

At first the chemicals were applied in low quantities (a total of 281,000 gallons) and within a limited geographical area. Then an air force team known as "Project Ranch Hand" was assigned to spray heavy applications of the most potent defoliant, Agent Orange. Ranch Hand missions became increasingly frequent, and from 1962 onward Agent Orange was the most widely produced and dispensed defoliant in Vietnam.

Broken promises, indiscriminate use

When the spraying was approved, the U.S. military had promised to avoid civilian populations, or at least to relocate civilians and resupply food in areas where herbicides had destroyed crops. But these promises were never kept. In 1965, forty-five percent of total spraying was aimed specifically at destroying crops, and no measures were taken to compensate civilians whose food supply had been obliterated. Initial targets were the forests and jungles around Saigon, the capital of South Vietnam, but eventually the geographic area was widened.

By 1967 so much Agent Orange was being sprayed that the U.S. chemical industry could not supply enough to meet rapidly growing demands. At this point the air force and the joint chiefs of staff (a group composed of the heads of all U.S. military services) took over the herbicide program. The Department of Defense was placed in charge of production and distribution of Agent Orange, which the government had by then diverted solely to military purposes. Commercial producers were encouraged to expand their facilities, build new plants, and work closely with the military. Certain chemical companies even sent technical advisors to Vietnam to show military personnel how to use the herbicide.

Vietnam heavily damaged

During the peak of Agent Orange spraying, around 1965, the air assault was massive. Twenty-four UC-123B aircraft flew approximately one hundred and twenty-nine sorties (flights), an average of thirty-nine per day, per airplane. The aircraft were joined by C-123 cargo carriers and helicopters. On the ground, the aircraft were supported by troops, trucks, and heavy equipment. In the case of dense jungle growth, the planes sprayed two applications of the herbicide—one for the upper layers of vegetation and the other for the lower layers. Agent Orange was used in undiluted (very concentrated) form, at the rate of three to four gallons per acre. This concentration is higher than was recommended by the military's own manual and far more than had ever been used commercially.

Overall, until 1971, a total of seventeen to nineteen million gallons of the liquid acid was sprayed on at least ten percent of the total land in Vietnam. (The Vietnamese government claims more than forty-four percent of the land was sprayed.) Sections of both Laos and Cambodia (neighboring countries involved in the war) were also secretly sprayed. As a result of this massive campaign, Agent Orange was very effective. Studies show that the chemical killed and defoliated ninety to ninety-five percent of the treated vegetation. For instance, thirty-six percent of all mangrove forests in South Vietnam were destroyed, revealing military targets such as Viet Cong tunnel openings, caves, and aboveground shelters.

Troops exposed to toxic chemicals

Although the military claimed success, the spraying missions took a tremendous toll on the people assigned to Agent Orange operations. Computer tapes now available show that some areas were sprayed as many as twenty-five times in just a few short months. Thus Agent Orange spraying sorties became highly dangerous, and there was a dramatic increase in exposure of troops in the air and on the ground. Helicopters flew without cargo doors so gunners could return heavy ground fire from the enemy, who were hiding under the dense jungle canopy. As Agent Orange was being sprayed, helicopter rotary blades kicked up gusts of chemicals, delivering a powerful dose onto the faces and bodies of the men inside the plane. On the ground, soldiers inhaled the misty chemical spray or splashed through puddles of Agent Orange that had spilled down upon them during emergency dumping.

Readily absorbing the herbicide into their skin and lungs, hundreds of thousands of troops were heavily exposed to toxic chemicals. Their bases, living quarters, and drinking water were contaminated with Agent Orange. They ate food that had been saturated with spray and swam or washed in herbicide-polluted water in bomb craters and rivers. Troops also inhaled fumes from empty fifty-five-gallon Agent Orange drums that had been improperly stored or carelessly tossed aside.

Air Force pilots who flew the Ranch Hand missions had the most direct contact with toxic chemicals, yet others were also consistently exposed. Among them were army pilots who involved in helicopter spraying, as well as navy and even marine pilots who were part of support units. Truck drivers were in constant contact with Agent Orange, for they transported the herbicide in the fifty-five-gallon drums that became familiar fixtures in base camps. Specialized mechanics, electricians, and technicians were indirectly exposed when they worked on aircraft that had been repeatedly contaminated.

Dioxin's legacy

After the United States withdrew its military forces from Vietnam in the early 1970s, returning veterans began noticing several medical problems for which they had few answers. In 1978 the Columbia Broadcasting System (CBS-TV) television network aired a program that exposed the dangers of Agent Orange. Immediately, chemical companies, the Veterans Administration, and the military made the decision to deny any relationship between the chemicals and these increasing health problems. Millions of dollars in potential compensation were at stake; as a result, the official Agent Orange cover-up began.

Dow leads coverup

The Dow Chemical Corporation coverup actually began in the early 1960s, when defoliants were first used in Vietnam. An Agent Orange manufacturer, Dow was aware that 2,4,5-T (one of the two basic ingredients in Agent Orange) had contained a toxic but unidentified chemical since 1937. By 1965—at the peak of spraying in Vietnam—Dow had identified the contaminant as dioxin, the most deadly known chemical substance. The company feared that if this fact was revealed, however, a congressional investigation would result in restrictions on the manufacture of pesticides with high dioxin content.

Dow took steps to conceal the truth. Calling together representatives of other Agent Orange manufacturers, Dow officials admitted that dioxin was dangerously toxic. In addition, the officials reported that one sign of dioxin exposure was chloracne (a skin eruption resembling acne). The appearance of chloracne was also an indication that a person's entire body was poisoned. Reports from the 1965 meeting indicate that Dow had required its own employees to take extreme precautions in handling the materials.

Rather than sharing this information with the military, however, Dow and its fellow contractors agreed among themselves to keep dioxin contamination low. A first step was controlling temperatures during the manufacturing process. The chemical companies also determined a safe exposure level: They acknowledged one part dioxin per million to be a significant health hazard. The problem was that in Vietnam, dioxin toxicity had varied from many parts per billion to many parts per million, depending on the individual production methods of each manufacturer. After the war, the U.S. military declared that contamination of up to 40,000 parts dioxin per billion was considered "unacceptable." But none of this information was available to the general public, and certainly it had never been relayed to Vietnam veterans.

Controversy erupts

In spite of the cover-up, the CBS-TV broadcast sparked controversy that in turn prompted numerous studies of Agent Orange. The government itself, in the form of the Environmental Protection Agency (EPA), played an important role in revealing the truth about Agent Orange. For instance, the EPA evacuated Times Beach, Missouri, when tests revealed soil samples there with two parts dioxin per billion. The EPA eventually stated that one part per billion is dangerous to humans. Years later, studies showed that dioxin could be toxic at drastically lower dosages.

The facts about the dioxin legacy continued to mount. A government research group that monitored dioxin—the Agency for Toxic Substances and Disease Registry Toxicological Profile for Dioxin—produced enough evidence to "conclude that dioxin deserves our greatest respect." According to a congressional report, "[dioxin] is classified as class six, super toxic

DIOXIN—A DEADLY SUBSTANCE

Dioxin (sometimes called "TCDD") has been studied in some manner—mostly in animal trials—in laboratories since the 1940s. Limited studies on dioxin-exposed people have also been conducted. The most recent information indicates that dioxin appears capable of interfering with a number of physiological (living body function) systems. EPA scientists and other researchers have called TCDD the most carcinogenic (cancer causing) compound ever studied. During the late 1980s and early 1990s, dioxin's potential to cause rare forms of cancer in humans—including soft tissue sarcoma and non-Hodgkin's lymphoma—was confirmed.

The EPA considers dioxin in food one million times more toxic than other deadly chemicals such as cadmium or arsenic. Recent EPA studies indicate that low-level dioxin exposure leads to reproductive system problems and immune system damage. (A deficient immune system leaves the body less able to defend itself against hostile forces in the natural environment.) It appears to be most damaging to young animals exposed in utero (in the womb). Reportedly, dioxin exposure also affects behavior and learning ability in humans, suggesting that it is neurotoxic (dangerous to the nervous system).

in a range of one [practically non-toxic] to six. [Dioxin] may be the most toxic and potent teratogen [an agent that causes developmental malformations] known to man based on toxicological data in guinea pigs and rabbits." Barry Commoner, director of the Center for the Biology of Natural Systems at Washington University in St. Louis, Missouri, also studied the chemical. According to Commoner, dioxin is "so potent a killer that just three ounces of it placed in New York City's water supply could wipe out the populace."

Children most affected

These studies also confirm what some Vietnam veterans have believed all along—that dioxin affects reproduction. Unusually high numbers of children with birth defects and delayed development have been born to dioxin-exposed veterans and to exposed Vietnamese mothers. A long-term, twenty-one-year study conducted in Vietnam identified spontaneous abortions, stillbirths, and birth defects as direct results of exposure to dioxin. Recent studies on infants born to mothers eating dioxin-contaminated fish also found that the infants had more than a ten percent decline in visual recognition memory.

Cancer, disease, unknown victims

When the American Legion (a veterans organization) conducted its own studies on Vietnam veterans, it concluded that at least thirty types of cancer and other diseases were related to the dioxin contaminant in Agent Orange. In 1993 the National Academy of Science's Institute of Medicine announced that dioxin could be linked to Hodgkin's disease and a skin-blistering condition known as porphyria cutanea tarda. Veterans suffering from these disorders, along with veterans who suffer two rare cancers and chloracne, have finally been acknowledged by the Veterans Administration as acceptable for compensation. All other medically damaged veterans and their birth-defective children have been ignored. In the meantime, thousands of exposed veterans have already died.

FOR FURTHER REFERENCE

Periodicals

Schmidt, K. F. "Dioxin's Other Face: Portrait of an Environmental Hormone." *Science News.* January 11, 1992, pp. 24–27.

Tschirley, F. "Dioxin." *Scientific American.*, February 1986, pp. 29–35.

The *Apollo 13* Oxygen Tank Rupture

APRIL 13, 1970

The *Apollo 13* mission had all the characteristics of a great misadventure, including overconfidence, disaster, and triumph.

On April 13, 1970, two days after the three-man crew of *Apollo 13* had been launched toward the Moon, an oxygen tank explosion disabled the spacecraft. This mishap forced the astronauts to abandon their mission of landing on the Moon and undertake a dangerous voyage back to Earth. The *Apollo 13* mission had all the characteristics of a great misadventure, including overconfidence, disaster, and triumph. This failed endeavor followed the highly successful manned lunar landing flights of *Apollo 11* and *Apollo 12* that were launched by the National Aeronautics and Space Administration (NASA) in the 1960s. The *Apollo 13* mission was even more ambitious than the previous lunar flights, since two moonwalks were scheduled. What is ironic about the *Apollo 13* misadventure is that even though the mission was a disaster, it was not a total failure. NASA personnel learned just how good they were at improvising solutions and preserving the lives of their astronauts. Unfortunately, as a result of the incident, the Apollo program was reduced.

Unlucky 13

The *Apollo 13* spacecraft was made up of two modules (independent units that are a part of the total structure of a space vehicle), the paired command and service modules

(CSM). The former module housed the crew, and the latter contained the engine and supply systems. The independent lunar module was attached to the command and service modules. This third module was designed to be used for the Moon landings while the CSM continued orbiting around the Moon. The lunar module would then blast off from the Moon, relink to the command and service modules, and eventually be discarded.

The crew was commanded by James A. Lovell (1928–), who was a veteran of two Gemini missions and of the first flight around the Moon, *Apollo 8.*. He was joined by two rookie astronauts: Fred W. Haise, who would pilot the lunar module, and John L. Swigert, the command module pilot. Swigert was a last-minute replacement for Thomas K. Mattingly, who had been exposed to German measles. The *Apollo 13* flight seemed to both test and confirm the bad luck traditionally associated with the number thirteen. The thirteenth Apollo voyage, the craft was launched at the thirteenth minute of the thirteenth hour of the day, Houston (Texas) time. On April 13, two days after its launch, the sudden crisis occurred.

"Houston, we've got a problem."

The accident that disabled the *Apollo 13* spacecraft took place in the initial part of the mission, approximately 56 hours and 205,000 miles into the flight. The astronauts heard a bang that was followed by a pressure drop in the service module's oxygen tanks and, correspondingly, in the command module. John Swigert matter-of-factly reported the malfunction in the service module oxygen tanks by saying "Houston, we've got a problem." No one in the spacecraft or at the NASA base in Houston understood why the oxygen pressure gauge for tank two soon read "zero" and the needle to the tank one gauge was dropping.

Thirteen minutes after the bang, the *Apollo 13* crew noticed a white, wispy cloud beginning to surround the service module. They correctly guessed that the cloud was their oxygen. An oxygen supply was vital to the mission—both for the crew to breathe and for the fuel cells in the service module to produce electrical power and water. The oxygen's uncontrolled venting explained not only the loss in pressure, but the spacecraft's tendency to keep veering off course. The spacecraft would, in addition, gradually be encircled by debris from the explosion.

The *Apollo 13* flight crew. The accident that disabled the spacecraft took place in the initial part of the mission, approximately 56 hours and 205,000 miles into the flight.

Backup systems are insufficient

The controllers in Houston were still struggling to interpret what their telemetry (data transmission) was telling them. The data seemed to indicate that the built-in redundancy (backup systems) of the Apollo spacecraft was turning out to be insufficient. But at this point no one could imagine that the spacecraft was actually undergoing the loss of a double redundancy system: two fuel cells and two oxygen tanks. Nor did anyone realize that a serious explosion had taken place. The problem was attributed instead to some sort of system breakdown or failure.

Despite this lack of understanding of what had transpired, it was evident to both Houston and the *Apollo 13* crew that the central command and service modules were becoming inoperative. About one hour and fifteen minutes after the accident, the only possible course of action became clear. The command and service modules had to be shut down since they only had about fifteen minutes' worth of power left, without which the spacecraft could not return to Earth. Thus, the crew was forced to deactivate the two modules and power the lunar module for use as a survival craft. This "lifeboat" option had been anticipated by the builders of the Apollo spacecraft, but no one had ever tested or fallen back on this strategy.

NASA improvises

Once the crew transferred into the small lunar module, the NASA controllers in Houston had to improvise nearly every procedure that enabled the three astronauts to survive during the spacecraft's voyage back to Earth. The lunar module was designed for the use of two men for thirty-three to thirty-five hours. This emergency required that it accommodate three men for up to one hundred hours. Houston also had to calculate how to use the lunar module's thrust engines to propel a complex spacecraft configuration.

All power, oxygen, and water supplies on the lunar module had to be strictly rationed. Power consumption was reduced to one-fifth of the normal level. Conserving power in part meant allowing the spacecraft's temperature to drop to a near-freezing thirty-eight degrees Fahrenheit. As it got colder inside the modules, the humidity rose and frost formed on the inside of the windows. The cold became almost unbearable, and Haise developed a kidney infection that plagued him for the rest of the trip.

A buildup of carbon dioxide (a gas formed from respiration) was an equally serious threat. The lithium hydroxide canisters (filters) in the lunar module could not remove all the carbon dioxide that three men would produce. After the equivalent canisters from the command module were found useless because they were differently-shaped, the crew devised a makeshift system to neutralize the carbon dioxide. The astronauts also were restricted to six ounces of water each per day. While starvation was not an issue, the food packs could not be reconstituted, because there was no hot water. In addition, no waste was ejected into space for fear that any venting might affect the spacecraft's delicate trajectory (path of travel) back to earth.

The navigation of the crippled spacecraft required its own set of improvisations. Once the craft reached the far side of the Moon, the lunar module's engines had to be fired very precise-

WHY DID THE OXYGEN TANK EXPLODE? As one NASA official put it, *Apollo 13* reminded everyone that "flying to the Moon is not just a bus ride." The explosion that took place during the mission was thoroughly investigated and a report was released in June 1970. The report revealed that a heater in an oxygen tank in the service module's fuel cells had exploded, bursting both oxygen tanks, the main engine, and all of the fuel cells. The cause was identified as defective thermostat switches that evidently had been damaged several years before the flight. Resulting heat buildup had welded the switches and burned the insulation off the wiring. The explosion occurred when the *Apollo 13* crew turned on the stirring fan in the oxygen tank.

ly to free the spacecraft from the Moon's gravitational pull and send it back toward Earth. Once this maneuver was accomplished, three other engine firings were crucial to speeding the craft's return to Earth and correcting its course.

The execution of these mid-course corrections was delicate and tense, since the debris from the original explosion now encircled the spacecraft like a cloud and gleamed in the Sun. This glittering debris made it impossible to find the familiar guide stars that the astronauts could have used for navigation and calculation of proper alignment. The NASA personnel in Houston, however, were able to conduct simulations and devise new strategies to navigate the craft.

Crew prepares for reentry

With each day that the *Apollo 13* spacecraft came closer to Earth, the NASA controllers became more concerned about the physical state of the crew. In addition to the cold and the shortage of oxygen and water, there was no place to sit or recline in the lunar module, which had only standing room for two men. A third crew member, therefore, was forced to spend periods of time trying to sleep in the even colder command module. Houston later learned that none of the crew had more than twelve hours of sleep in the three and one-half days it took to return to Earth. NASA was particularly worried about the effects of fatigue, cold, and dehydration (depletion of bodily fluids) on the crew's efficiency, since the astronauts would soon have to copy down correctly an emergency checklist of procedures and commands read to them from Houston. This task alone would take two hours.

Through these commands—which specified hundreds of switch, valve, and dial positions—the *Apollo 13* crew readied their craft for the final reentry and splashdown. When still several hours from Earth, they attempted the crucial power-up of the command module. It was this module that contained the heat-shielded capsule designed to protect the men during the fiery reentry into Earth's atmosphere. If the crew could not activate this module, they would be left stranded in space. Fortunately, the power-up worked, and for the first time in days the astronauts began to feel warm.

A highly accurate splashdown

On April 17, five hours before the splashdown, the lunar module's thrust engines were fired a final time to start the reentry. Half an hour later, the crew used explosive charges to get rid of the damaged service module. As it drifted away from them, the astronauts photographed the extent of the damage the service module had suffered. Swigert exclaimed, "There's one whole side of that spacecraft missing!" Then the three astronauts left the lunar module for the last time. Once inside the command module, ninety minutes before reentry, the astronauts cast off what had served as their lifeboat.

The remaining module was soon reentering the Earth's atmosphere. As it streaked through at some 25,000 miles per hour, the heat shield (which ground controllers feared had been damaged in the explosion) was able to withstand a temperature of 4,000 degrees Fahrenheit. After an unusually long period out of contact, the capsule parachuted down within full view of the *Iwo Jima*, a U.S. carrier. Remarkably, *Apollo 13* benefitted from one of the most accurate splashdowns and the fastest crew-recovery operation in the history of the Apollo program. Once rescued, the exhausted astronauts were barely able to stand on the *Iwo Jima's* deck. Lovell had lost fourteen pounds, Haise still had a severe kidney infection, and all three men were badly dehydrated. But, despite the odds, they had survived.

Apollo program cut back

The *Apollo 13* crisis showed that thousands of NASA and space industry personnel could cooperate to solve an unprecedented and complex technical dilemma, with three lives hanging in the balance all the while. Nonetheless, the accident made many observers question the need for repeated manned lunar landings. In addition to causing a nearly ten-month delay in NASA's timetable, the *Apollo 13* oxygen tank rupture led to the reduction of the Apollo program by three missions. *Apollo 18, Apollo 19,* and *Apollo 20* were all canceled in the wake of budget cuts imposed by Congress.

FOR FURTHER REFERENCE

Books

Cole, Michael D. *Apollo 13: Space Emergency.* Springfield, NJ: Enslow Publishing, 1995.

Lovell, Jim, and Jeffrey Kluger. *Lost Moon: The Perilous Voyage of Apollo 13.* New York City: Houghton Mifflin, 1994.

Ford Pinto Rear-Impact Defect

1971 TO 1976

Soon after its debut in 1971, the Ford Pinto became the hottest subcompact (small car) automobile on the market. Over the Pinto's nine-year lifespan, more than three million of the vehicles were sold. By the middle of the 1970s, however, reports began to surface that the Pinto tended to catch fire after rear-impact collisions. *Mother Jones* magazine and the Center for Automotive Safety maintained that design flaws in the vehicle made its fuel tank system vulnerable and hazardous. In 1978 Ford recalled 1.4 million Pintos made between 1971 and 1976 for safety modifications. By the mid-1980s, at least 59 people had burned to death in Pinto accidents, resulting in more than 100 lawsuits against Ford.

The magazine *Mother Jones* accused Ford executives of deciding against Pinto safety modifications because "it wasn't profitable to make the changes."

Car rushed into production

Because the Pinto was the Ford Motor Company's first significant entry into the small-car market, the vehicle was rushed into production. The typical forty-three-month development phase for a new automobile was reportedly abbreviated to as few as twenty-five months. Ford began building the car early in the schedule, before the quality assurance process was complete. Even though Ford had been a safety pioneer in the mid-1950s, offering such innovations as seatbelts, it retreated from those standards for the subcompact Pinto. "Safety doesn't sell"

This 1973 Ford Pinto was struck from behind, causing a deadly fire. Soon after its 1971 debut, the Ford Pinto became the most popular small car on the market.

was a common attitude among automobile manufacturers at the time. Ford was also charged with employing a series of delaying tactics to fight a proposed safety rule—Federal Motor Vehicle Safety Standard 301—that could have compelled the automaker to redesign the Pinto.

"Import fighter" criticized for flaws

The initial sales figures for the Pinto were good news for Ford chairman Lee Iacocca, who had spearheaded development of the vehicle as an "import fighter." (At the time foreign-made, or import, small cars were selling well in the United States.) Iacocca's goal was a sensible "econocar" priced under $2,000 and weighing less than 2,000 pounds.

Ford and Iacocca were praised for the success of the automobile. Then the Center for Automotive Safety, a group run by disciples of consumer advocate Ralph Nader, began receiving complaints about the Pinto. According to these reports, the cars' fuel tanks were easily punctured in a rear-impact crash, setting off a fire that could kill or seriously burn the occupants of the car.

Center demands action

The Center for Automotive Safety demanded government action. In the fall of 1977 the National Highway Traffic Safety Administration initiated a "defects investigation" of the Pinto. Around the same time *Mother Jones,* a San Francisco-based investigative magazine, unleased a bombshell against Ford. A lengthy article revealed that the development phase for the Pinto had been accelerated. The article pinpointed flaws in the vehicle's fuel-tank structure, particularly its vulnerable position in the rear. Even more damaging was the assertion, based on previously concealed corporate documents, that Ford executives knew Pintos were prone to catch fire after rear-end collisions.

Ford knew about flaws

Ford documents revealed that early Pintos had been tested more than forty times. Engineers had discovered ruptures or leaks in the fuel tank after rear-end collisions at twenty-one and a half miles per hour. Ford's testing continued after the Pinto was in production. A report on fuel tanks in 1971–72 Pinto models concluded that rear-end placement was unsatisfactory for a twenty-mile-per-hour crash. Major design changes were needed for the Pinto to withstand a thirty-mile-per-hour collision.

Ford documents also revealed proposals to improve the Pinto's rear-end safety. These proposals included repositioning the tank, moving the filler pipe, shielding protruding parts, and installing a bladder in the tank. The most effective of the solutions might have been placing the fuel tank above the rear axle. Ironically, Ford held a patent on that type of tank, and used it on the European-built Capri, which was imported to the United States. Soon after the Pinto's debut, the Capri passed the equivalent of a rear-end crash test at forty-five miles per hour. British ads even boasted of the Capri tank's safety.

Ford defends Pinto

In spite of finding these flaws, Ford vigorously defended the Pinto. The company argued that the fuel system presented no unreasonable risk. Ford officials insisted that, in addition to meeting government safety requirements, the Pinto was as safe as other vehicles of its size and type. The Pinto did meet federal standards, but until 1977 cars were not required to withstand a rear-end collision of a specific force.

Government intervenes

In October 1976, the NHTSA ordered the recall of 372,584 Ford cars, including Pintos, Bobcats, and Mustang II models. The reason for the recall was potential fuel leaks. By 1978 NHTSA investigations found that rear-end collisions at low to moderate speeds resulted in the leaking or rupturing of Pinto fuel tanks. The NHTSA further determined that fuel leaks could "result in fire." Moreover, government experts knew of thirty-eight cases of fuel tank damage, leakage, and fires that resulted in twenty-six fatalities.

Ford announces "voluntary recall"

On June 15, 1978, shortly before a public hearing that probably would have forced a recall, Ford announced a "voluntary" recall of 1.4 million 1971 to 1976 model Pintos. (The Pinto fuel tank had been redesigned beginning with the 1977 edition.) The company also recalled thirty thousand similar 1975 to 1976 model Mercury Bobcats. Ford did not admit to the existence of a defect, but agreed to make changes to "end public concern." The changes included placing two heavy polyethylene shields around the fuel tank. Consumer advocate Nader called this remedy "an inadequate technical fix; the cheapest way out." Nader wanted Ford to install a double-wall tank like the one used on bigger Fords.

Lawsuits are filed

Ford undoubtedly hoped the Pinto controversy would fade after the recall. The company, however, was swamped with lawsuits. Among them was a sensational Indiana case that focused national attention on the Pinto. In August 1978, three teenage girls died when their 1973 Pinto burst into flames after being struck from the rear by a van. As the Indiana case opened in 1980, Ford was facing more than fifty civil suits and at least two class-action suits (litigation brought on behalf of a group of peo-

GENERAL MOTORS RECALLS PICKUP TRUCKS Allegations that American-made vehicles represent fire and safety hazards did not end with the Ford Pinto. In the early 1990s, the Center for Auto Safety charged that almost five million 1973 to 1987 General Motors pickup trucks were fire-prone in side-impact collisions. The cause was the "sidesaddle" placement of the trucks' fuel tanks. The National Highway Traffic Safety Administration pressured General Motors to recall and modify the affected trucks. Various civil lawsuits and thirty-six class-action suits were filed against General Motors. In February 1993, an Atlanta, Georgia, jury awarded $105.2 million to the family of a teenager killed in a General Motors pickup.

ple). Courts had already awarded plaintiffs (people who brought suits against Ford) as much as six million dollars in damages.

With the Indiana trial Ford earned the dubious distinction of being the first corporation charged with a criminal offense— reckless homicide. Ford was eventually acquitted of the charges by the trial's presiding judge, Harold Staffeldt. The judge said he was troubled that the case represented "a revolt against technology" instead of a complaint against a specific design flaw. Despite Ford's acquittal, the negative publicity surrounding the Indiana case was extremely damaging, and consumer advocates continued to lobby against the car. The Pinto gradually began dropping out of the market. It was replaced in 1981 by the Ford Escort.

Dollars before lives

The controversy surrounding the Pinto created widespread public distrust of the American automotive industry. Most damaging was the allegation that Ford cold-bloodedly put dollars ahead of lives. *Mother Jones* accused Ford executives of deciding against safety modifications because "it wasn't profitable to make the changes." This charge was supported by documented proof. In 1966 the National Traffic and Motor Vehicle Safety Act gave Ford the right to conduct what is called a "cost-benefit analysis." The analysis was a way to determine whether it would be more profitable to correct design flaws or simply make lawsuit settlements.

Ford reportedly used the results of a cost-benefit analysis when the company decided not to install a fuel valve in certain vehicles. This is how the analysis worked: Company analysts estimated that unless changes were made, 2,100 vehicles would eventually burn, causing 180 deaths and 180 serious injuries. The analysts placed monetary values at $200,000 per death, $67,000 per injury, and $700 per vehicle. The total for all this came to $49.5 million, which was the amount Ford could expect to pay in lawsuits.

The next step was to calculate the cost of modifying the Pintos. Analysts concluded this latter amount would be considerably higher, around $137 million. By not making the safety modification, Ford could save $87.5 million. Similarly, Ford did not correct the Pinto fuel-tank problem because doing so would have cost more than the company estimated it would pay out in accident-related lawsuits. (The estimated cost of modifying the fuel tank was $10 to $15 per car.) In the end, corporate profit took priority over the saving of lives.

FOR FURTHER REFERENCE

Books

Lacey, Robert. *Ford: The Men and the Machine*. New York City: Little, Brown, 1986.

Three Mile Island Meltdown

MARCH 28, 1979

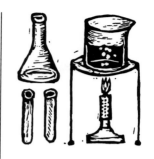

O n March 28, 1979, a partial meltdown occurred at Unit 2 of the Three Mile Island nuclear power plant in Middletown, Pennsylvania. A valve in a pipe carrying cooling water, which was supposed to be closed, accidentally remained stuck in the "open" position. Cooling water was then allowed to flow out of the reactor. Heat built up within the reactor core, causing some fuel elements to melt, releasing radioactive gas and water into the surrounding environment. No one was killed or injured, but expert opinion remains divided about possible future health problems that might result from the incident. The Three Mile Island accident—and its potential aftereffects—was a critical factor in the dramatic decrease in use of nuclear power in the United States after 1979.

Operated by several power companies

The Three Mile Island nuclear power plant consisted of two units that sat on a small island in the middle of the Susquehanna River in south-central Pennsylvania. Unit 1 (or TMI-1) was put into operation in September 1974. Construction on Unit 2 (or TMI-2) began in 1968 and was completed in 1978. (The unit's formal opening date was December 30, 1978.) Both of these units were built by Babcock & Wilcox, a giant construction company that specialized in nuclear power plant

The Three Mile Island accident was a critical factor in the dramatic decrease in the use of nuclear power in the United States after 1979.

The Three Mile Island nuclear power plant. The 1979 plant accident has had an negative impact on the use of nuclear power in the United States.

components. The Three Mile Island complex was owned by a consortium (cooperating group) of power companies—Pennsylvania Electric Company, Jersey Central Power and Light Company, and Metropolitan Edison.

How a nuclear reactor works

The Three Mile Island units were pressurized-water reactors, the most commonly used nuclear reactors in the United States. In a water reactor, heat is generated in the core when

| Great Misadventures

neutrons bombard uranium atoms in fuel rods, which causes fission (splitting atoms and releasing energy) to occur. The TMI-2 unit had 36,816 fuel rods, each filled with hundreds of pellets of enriched uranium metal about the size and shape of a small checker.

Heat produced by the fission reaction is removed by cooling water that is pumped through the reactor core. The cooling water is then pumped out of the core to a heat exchanger, where it is used to boil water in a secondary system. Steam that is produced in the secondary system is used to drive turbines (a type of engine) that turn electric generators. At peak capacity, the Three Mile Island plant produced 880 megawatts of electricity. This was enough electricity to meet the needs of the 346,000 residents in surrounding Berks, Lebanon, and York counties in Pennsylvania.

Has problems despite safety system

Like all nuclear power plants, the Three Mile Island reactors contained a complex safety system with many backup components. The core itself was enclosed in a steel casing almost nine inches thick. The core and cooling system, in turn, were enclosed within a large containment dome that measured 190 feet in height and 140 feet in diameter. The reinforced concrete walls of the dome were four feet thick. The purpose of the containment dome was to capture any gases, radiation, or other materials released during a leak or accident in the core or the cooling system.

Although TMI-2 was carefully designed, a number of problems began occurring almost from the day it was licensed in February 1978. During the test period, valves opened and closed when they were not supposed to and they remained stuck in the wrong position. Seals broke, recording instruments failed to work properly, and other "glitches" developed. The situation did not improve even after the plant became officially operational in December 1978. The unit had been running only two weeks when two safety valves failed, causing the plant to shut down for two more weeks. During February, additional problems with valves, seals, pumps, and instruments developed. The plant seemed jinxed by one mishap after another.

ACCIDENT PRODUCED
WIDESPREAD EFFECTS In the
immediate area surrounding the Three Mile
Island complex, residents became—and have
remained—concerned about the possible
effects of the meltdown on their health.
Given the nature of short-term radiation, it
is possible that increased rates of cancer or
birth defects may not show up for years. A
reflection of these concerns are the more
than 2,200 lawsuits that have been filed by
area residents because of the accident. To
date, 280 claims have been settled at a total
cost of about $14 million dollars.

Operations at Unit 1 were significantly
affected by the events at the neighboring
Unit 2 reactor. More than one hundred
modifications were made in Unit 1, at a cost
of $95 million. To complete the necessary
renovations, the plant was shut down for six
years. During that time, an improved and
expanded training program for unit
personnel was developed and implemented.
Much of the training at the plant is now
done in an $18 million, full-scale replica of
the Unit 1 control room. The Unit 2
accident was also the subject of a number of
investigations and studies. Probably the most
important documents were the Rogovin
Report, which was issued by the Nuclear
Regulatory Commission (NRC), and the
Kemeny Report, which was commissioned
by President Jimmy Carter. As a result of
these studies, in 1980 the NRC issued new
regulations requiring modifications of existing
and future plans for nuclear plants.

The problem is that experts still disagree about the health effects of low-level radiation. A person receives about twenty millirems of radiation from a typical chest X ray, so the levels measured at TMI-2 seemed reasonably safe. Some authorities, however, believe that each additional dose of radiation, no matter how small, increases a person's chance of contracting cancer later in life.

Cleanup begins

Cleanup efforts on the damaged reactor began almost immediately. The immediate source of concern was the steam-hydrogen bubble in the containment dome. Engineers vented (released) part of the gas into the atmosphere through filters that removed its radioactivity. The engineers were also able to transfer some of the steam-hydrogen mixture to an outside building where the hydrogen was combined chemically with oxygen to make water. Cleanup crews were able to remove twenty thousand gallons of radioactive water that had flowed into the auxiliary building by transferring it to holding tanks.

Finally, a variety of methods were used to cool down the hot reactor core itself, preventing any further meltdown.

The long-term cleanup of TMI-2 was a slow, dangerous, and complex process that took eleven years. Eventually one hundred fifty metric tons of damaged fuel rods and other reactor components were shipped to the Idaho National Engineering Laboratory for storage and analysis. The total cost of the cleanup process was $973 million.

There are no plans to repair TMI-2. Safety experts will continue to observe and monitor the plant until early into the twenty-first century. At that point, the unit will be shut down, along with the TMI-1. By then the maintenance costs are projected to reach nearly $2 billion—without the reactor ever producing any significant amount of electricity.

Public opposes nuclear power

As a result of the Three Mile Island accident, the nuclear power industry became more involved in safety issues. For instance, power companies established the Institute of Nuclear Power Operations (INPO) to review, evaluate, and improve nuclear power plant performance. An even more profound result, however, was a decrease in the use of nuclear power in the United States. Orders for nuclear power plants had already begun to decline in the year preceding the TMI-2 event.

Three Mile Island also marked a turning point in the public's attitude toward nuclear power. Citing the partial meltdown as a near-worst-case scenario for a nuclear catastrophe, activists campaigned against plants already under development. They also worked to defeat plans for new plants. Those efforts have been largely successful. Since 1979 no new nuclear plants have been ordered, and plans for fifty-nine reactors have been canceled. Seventeen new plants have been opened, but all of them were in final stages of planning or construction at the time of the Three Mile Island accident.

FOR FURTHER REFERENCE

Books

Gray, Mike, and Ira Rosen. *The Warning: Accident at Three Mile Island.* New York City: Norton, 1982.

MGM Grand Hotel Fire

NOVEMBER 21, 1980

The MGM Grand Hotel fire raised the question: What is more important—saving buildings or saving lives?

Sparks from a short-circuit started a fire in the MGM Grand Hotel in Las Vegas, Nevada, on November 21, 1980. Despite having passed several inspections, the building's fire protection systems could not prevent the fire from engulfing the hotel in smoke and flames. Thick black smoke filled air ducts, guest rooms, and escape stairwells. Some people tried to escape by racing to the roof or running down smoke-filled stairwells. Other guests called for help or huddled near broken windows while smoke billowed into their rooms. Eighty-five people died and more than six hundred were injured in the fire, primarily due to smoke inhalation rather than the fire itself. The disaster dramatically increased the updating of fire code regulations for both new and existing high-rise buildings. It also raised an important question: What is more important, saving buildings or saving lives?

Specially designed fire protection system

The MGM Grand Hotel was an enormous facility. It housed a casino, two one-thousand-seat theaters, forty shops, five restaurants, over two thousand guest rooms, a jai alai fronton (court), and a sports arena. A T-shaped tower of guest rooms rose above two entertainment levels, each of which was as large as twenty football fields.

Prior to the disaster, the huge complex featured a safety system that was specially designed to protect it from fire. Alarms and other devices were installed for immediate action and alert. Fire zones and exit routes were built to contain a blaze and enable occupants to escape quickly. In addition, the heating, ventilation, and air conditioning (HVAC) system had been built to prevent the entry of oxygen, which feeds a blaze during a fire.

Hotel catches fire

Most of the people in the hotel at the time of the fire were casino gamblers, hotel guests, and MGM Grand employees. The fire started early in the morning in a delicatessen that had not yet opened for the day. Around 7:10 A.M. on November 21, 1980, an employee noticed sparks coming out of a board in the delicatessen. A chef tried to extinguish the fire, but soon was forced to flee the area. The fire fed on fresh air supplied by the HVAC system, as well as abundant combustible materials in the del-

A helicopter rescues guests from the roof of the burning MGM Grand Hotel in Las Vegas, Nevada.

icatessen. Soon heavy smoke was carrying unburned fuels. The fire then moved into the casino on the upper entertainment level and into the guest tower.

When the fire department arrived, flammable gases had collected in the "eye in the sky" above the casino (a network of walkways that allows security personnel to monitor gambling operations unnoticed). The fire quickly moved down to the casino floor. Firefighters later reported that they noticed a layer of smoke six to eight feet from the ceiling. Within approximately twelve seconds, the smoke had dropped to four feet above the floor. In a powerful firestorm, flames then burst through glass doors at the west end of the hotel.

Most of the guests and employees on the casino level were able to escape the building ahead of the fire. Some guests in the hotel tower, rather than attempting to evacuate down the stairwells, scrambled onto the roof. Many others remained in their

RETROFITTING TOO EXPENSIVE The damage scope of the MGM Grand Hotel fire may have been decreased if the owners had been required to meet retroactive fire codes. Such requirements state that existing buildings must be upgraded to comply with newly adopted fire-protection guidelines. Yet this process, which is called "retrofitting," involves large costs for building owners and communities. At the time of the MGM Grand Hotel fire, few retroactive fire codes were in effect in Las Vegas, Nevada.

rooms and broke or opened windows to gain access to fresh air. The fire department was able to control the fire by around 8:30 A.M. Helicopters were used to rescue nearly a thousand people from the fast-moving fire. By 11:00 A.M. the majority of survivors had been evacuated. Eighty-five people had died and more than six hundred were injured, primarily from smoke inhalation.

Inadequate fire protection systems

A full-scale investigation was conducted immediately after the fire. Investigators found that inadequacies and failures in the hotel's fire protection systems contributed to the disaster. First, the fire crippled the alarm system, preventing guests in the tower from receiving any warning. Fire zone enclosures then failed, allowing smoke to enter air ducts, elevator shafts, and stairways. Smoke soon filled the entire the building.

The HVAC system, rather than depriving the fire of oxygen, provided it with fresh air. A chimney effect, which was created by vertical passageways and the HVAC system, drew the smoke quickly up into guest tower hallways and rooms. Poor exit routes, however, proved to be the most deadly factor. Stairwells were the only paths of escape from the guest rooms to the street. Once hotel guests entered the stairwells, self-locking doors prevented people from returning to the hallways. As smoke filled the stairwells, many people became trapped. The only safety precaution that operated correctly was the automatic sprinkler system. The sprinklers prevented the fire from spreading into the guest tower or beyond casino-level areas that were not equipped with sprinklers.

Smoke rises from the MGM Grand Hotel as it burns on November 21, 1980. Despite numerous flaws in the hotel's protection systems, the MGM Grand was not in significant violation of current fire safety standards.

Poor construction fed fire

Investigators determined that several factors caused the fire protection systems at the MGM Grand Hotel to fail or perform inadequately. Foremost among these factors were construction deficiencies. When the complex was built in 1972, it had been designed to contain areas known as "fire zones." To create fire zones, sections of the building had been isolated by special walls made of fireproof materials to prevent the spread of fire and smoke and protect occupants and property. The walls were supposed to seal off openings between building parts and cover gaps between construction materials through which fire and smoke could pass.

Authorities discovered, however, that many fire zone enclosures in the hotel and casino had been left open or were covered with materials that could not resist fire or stop smoke. Elevator shafts were not even adequately vented. Materials that did not meet official fire-prevention standards had been used to build ceilings and attic areas. Decorations, furnishings, and other items in the casino contained high amounts of synthetic materials. Not only do synthetic materials easily catch fire and burn, but they also produce large amounts of smoke.

Fire dampers used improperly

As investigators sorted through the fire-damaged rubble of the MGM Grand Hotel, they found faulty fire dampers (hinged louvers similar to those on attic exhaust fans in many residences). Fire dampers, which are an important part of HVAC systems in large buildings, are installed near circulation fans where air crosses fire zones. The dampers are held open by a link designed to melt in the heat of a fire, thereby closing the louvers and stopping the flow of air. In this way, air is allowed to circulate through the building under normal circumstances while keeping the fire zone isolated at the same time. At the MGM Grand, however, some fire dampers had been bolted open or their "melt-down" links had been replaced with metal wire. Therefore the dampers were prevented from functioning properly.

Alarm systems failed

Many fatalities at the MGM Grand resulted from the failure of the fire suppression and alarm system that was designed to detect and control a fire. The fire suppression system was based on automatic water sprinklers located in selected portions of the building. The heat of a fire would set off these sprinklers. The minimum guidelines of the fire code in effect at the time of hotel's design did not require entire facility to be equipped with sprinklers. The assumption was that these areas would be open twenty-four hours a day and fire would be detected quickly. Thus, the casino, delicatessen, most floors in the guest tower, and many other areas were not protected by sprinklers. Most important, the fire suppression and alarm systems in these areas were entirely dependent on human detection in order to be activated.

An especially crucial unprotected area was the eye in the sky, where security personnel monitor gambling operations. The alarm system was designed so that someone who noticed an outbreak of fire could alert the hotel's security office. Security officers would verify the emergency, then use fire alarms

DISASTER PROMPTS NEW SMOKE DETECTORS More than ninety percent of the victims who died in the MGM Grand Hotel fire were overcome by smoke rather than flames. As a consequence of that event, several communities throughout the country increased the emphasis on smoke control in fire protection regulations. These changes represented a shift in priorities from saving buildings to saving lives. Among the corrective measures was perfecting smoke detectors that work in conjunction with air circulation systems. As soon as a smoke detector signals the presence of a fire, exhaust fans move air out of a fire area. At the same time, venting systems contain the circulation of smoke to keep it from moving into surrounding areas. Although fire protection professionals do not agree about the feasibility of all smoke control methods, many cities now require that high-rise buildings be equipped with smoke-control systems.

and public address systems to alert hotel and casino occupants to danger. At the time of the fire, however, spaces where the fire code did not require sprinklers had in fact been closed down during low-use periods. One such area was the delicatessen, where the fire started. Since the employees who noticed the fire had to flee for their lives, they were not able to notify the security office in a timely fashion. Consequently, precious moments passed before the officers became aware of the fire and sounded the alarm.

Protection system was outmoded

The MGM Grand fire was also the result of outmoded fire-protection systems. In the eight years between the design and construction of the hotel in 1972, and the fire on November 21, 1980, several advances in fire protection for high-rise buildings had been incorporated into Las Vegas fire codes. Among these advances were smoke detectors, refuge centers, direct connection of fire alarms to fire departments, communication systems for use by firefighters during a fire, and smoke exhaust systems. None of these measures had been required at the MGM Grand.

Leads to national fire code revision

The nation's second most deadly hotel fire provoked a flurry of discussions about fire protection. Despite numerous flaws in the hotel's protection systems, however, the MGM Grand was not in significant violation of safety standards at the time of the fire. In fact, only six months earlier the building had passed a fire inspection. The disaster brought several issues to the forefront. Among them were the danger of smoke as well as fire, and the failure of protection systems to be upgraded with new fire-prevention technology. The fire also led to a reexamination of the value placed on human life when communities encourage building development and economic expansion. Later fire codes gave the first priority to saving lives rather than protecting a building or an owner's financial investment. These reforms point to the important political significance of the MGM Grand Hotel disaster, which many regard as a misadventure that resulted from misplaced priorities.

FOR FURTHER REFERENCE

Periodicals

"Fire at the MGM Grand." *Fire Journal*. January, 1982, pp. 19–32.

The Superconducting Super Collider

EARLY 1980s TO 1993

The most expensive basic research project in history, the SSC seemed almost programmed for disaster.

In 1993 the U.S. Congress voted to end funding of the Superconducting Super Collider (also called the "SSC"), a gigantic machine designed to study elementary particles and forces. Housed in a fifty-three-mile, race-track-shaped tunnel 150 feet underground near Waxahachie, Texas, the SSC was designed to answer a question frequently posed by scientists: What is the fundamental nature of matter? The SSC was one of the most expensive research projects ever planned; in fact, its overall budget exceeded $11 billion. After six years of construction problems and cost overruns, however, the SSC was only twenty percent completed. Amounting to little more than an impressive hole in the ground, the SSC was a monumental failure. In 1993, after spending more than $2 billion, Congress appropriated (or assigned) $640 million to dismantle the project.

From linac to synchrotron

The concept of the SSC was based on the accelerator. The accelerator was invented around 1929 by Alabama-born physicist Robert Jemison Van de Graaf (1901-1967). (A physicist is a scientist who studies matter and energy and their interaction.) Van de Graaf's invention led initially to the development of the particle accelerator, then to increasingly more sophisticated devices. (A particle accelerator is a device used to increase the velocity [speed] of subatomic particles such as protons [particles with a positive charge], electrons [particles with a negative charge], and positrons [positively charged particles that contain an electron, or negatively charged, particle].)

The first of these more advanced mechanisms was the linear accelerator (or "linac"), which consists of a few hundred or a few thousand cylindrical metal tubes arranged one in front of the other. Within these tubes a particle is exposed to a series of electrical fields, each of which increases the velocity of the particle. The largest linac in the world is the Stanford Linear Accelerator, located at the Stanford Linear Accelerator Center (SLAC) in Stanford, California. At SLAC a two-mile underground tunnel passes beneath U.S. Highway 10 and holds 82,650 tubes along with magnetic, electrical, and auxiliary equipment needed for the machine's operation.

Since the linac was limited to operating in a straight line, engineers turned to developing machines that would accelerate particles in a circle. An early circular accelerator was the cyclotron, which was invented by University of California physics professor Ernest Orlando Lawrence (1901-1958) in the 1930s. By the 1950s scientists in various countries had built a number of machines based on the cyclotron. Among these machines was the synchrotron, which consisted of a hollow circular tube called the ring, through which particles were accelerated. The particles were first accelerated to velocities close to the speed of light in smaller machines, and then injected into the main ring. Once they were within the main ring, the particles received additional jolts of energy from accelerating chambers placed at various locations around the ring. Along this route very strong magnets controlled the path followed by the particles. As the particles picked up energy and tended to spiral outward, the magnetic fields were increased, pushing the particles back into a circular path. The most powerful synchrotrons now in operation can produce energies of at least 400 gigaelectron volts (GeV; a gigaelectron contains one billion electron volts).

Final key to the universe

In the 1970s nuclear physicists (scientists who study the nucleus of the atom) in the United States proposed the design

THE PARTICLE ACCELERATOR

Particle accelerators enable scientists to study the basic structure of matter. The original accelerator—created by Robert Van de Graaf in 1929—consisted of a silk conveyor belt that collected positive charges from a high-voltage source at the end of the belt. The charges were then transferred to a hollow dome located at the top of the machine at the other end of the belt. The Van de Graaf accelerator could be converted to a particle accelerator by attaching a source of positively charged ions (charged subatomic particles such as protons) to the dome. These ions felt an increasingly strong force of repulsion as positive charges accumulated in the dome. At some point, the ions were released from their source, and they travelled away from the dome with high energy and at high velocities. If this beam of rapidly moving particles was directed at a target, the ions collided with atoms in the target and broke them apart. An analysis of ion-atom collisions such as these provided substantial information about the structure of the atoms and the ion "bullets," as well as the nature of matter in general.

and construction of the most powerful synchrotron of all—the SSC. The researchers speculated that the SSC would provide answers to the unresolved mysteries of the universe. With each modification of Van de Graaf's accelerator, researchers had been able to acquire new knowledge about the forces that govern the universe. For instance, they discovered that all matter (a substance that occupies space and consists of atoms) consists of quarks (particles that come in pairs), leptons (particles that experience no strong force), and interacting forces. This concept, which is called the "Standard Model," is the closest man has ever come to defining the nature of matter. Nevertheless, deficiencies in the Standard Model led physicists to propose the SSC as a way to close gaps and answer remaining questions.

Biggest science project in history

When the idea for the SSC was introduced, critics were wary of the project, saying it would have no practical use and would therefore be a waste of taxpayers' money. Supporters touted the supercollider as the ultimate intellectual challenge. By the 1980s, SSC proponents had successfully lobbied for government funds and construction began. Originally budgeted at $4.4 billion, the SSC was to be the largest and most expensive scientific device ever built. The site chosen for the gigantic machine was near Waxahachie, Texas, twenty-five miles south of Dallas.

According to the plan, the SSC would consist of a 53-mile tunnel in the shape of a race track that was 10 feet in diameter and buried 150 feet underground. Nine thousand superconducting magnets would be placed in two ring formations on particle beam pipes within the tunnel. The magnets would focus, propel, and guide two beams of protons that are traveling in opposite directions. As the protons are propelled around the track, they would gain momentum with each circuit until they nearly reach the speed of light. During this process the protons would enter interaction halls, where they would cross over and collide with energy that is twenty times greater than any ever achieved by man. Researchers would use the force produced by this collision to re-create the birth of the universe and thus gain greater insight into the nature of matter.

Astronomical costs, minimal progress

The SSC may have been doomed from the outset. Although the venture had enough congressional support to reach the building stage, the American public did not understand why the SSC should be given top priority. Compounding this problem was the fact that the cost of the project had been severely underestimated. By 1993, six years after ground was broken for the tunnel, the price tag had escalated from $4.4 billion to $11 billion and construction had not advanced beyond the initial stages.

During the six years of construction, the SSC had been the subject of more than twelve audits and official investigations, many of which reported mismanagement and cost overruns. Rejecting these findings, SSC officials claimed the project had remained on schedule and within budget. At least $4 billion of the increased costs resulted, they said, from required technical changes and a three-year extension granted by President Bill Clinton. Unanticipated economic inflation had also strained the budget—a development that could not be blamed on SSC planners. But public and congressional patience with the barely understood dream of a few high-energy physicists had reached the breaking point.

Internal dissent, lack of support

Supporters of the supercollider tried to put the escalating costs in perspective by stressing the practical benefits. They pointed to the creation of jobs in superconducting technology and potential medical advances from the use of particle beams. Yet SSC advocates could not counter the criticism that came from the scientific community itself. Many physicists, for instance, said the SSC had been oversold and overrated. Another problem was that project planners had guaranteed international backing, but no other countries ever came forward to share the costs.

The SSC was finally scuttled, however, because it lacked congressional support. Members of Congress more or less turned their backs on the venture once most of the project contracts had been awarded in the state of Texas. No longer having a vested interest in winning money for their own constituents (residents in a congressional district), congressmen from other states had no reason to sustain the project. Congress was also facing a huge budget deficit—$300 billion—that made the SSC seem a frivolous waste of the nation's limited funds. On October 21, 1993, Congress voted 280 to 150 to eliminate the SSC and designated $640 million for the "orderly termination" of the project. The Department of Energy later set the final close-down date for January 1, 1995, after which the SSC Laboratory staff would be reduced to a skeleton crew.

Jobs lost, careers damaged

At the time of the congressional decision in 1993, the SSC involved more than 2,000 jobs. A 1,000-member scientific team built the $500 million Gamma-Electron-Muon detector (a device for detecting the presence of electromagnetic waves or radioactivity) and at least 1,000 scientific and technical employees worked on other aspects of the supercollider complex. When Congress voted to terminate the project, the decision not only had a devastating impact on the 2,000 people at the SSC Laboratory in Waxahachie, but it also produced long-range negative effects in Texas and throughout the nation.

Especially hard hit were universities, which had created entire higher-physics programs and departments with government grants for research on the SSC. In turn, the higher-physics profession itself was thrown into turmoil as jobs that had been generated by the SSC at contracting firms and commercial labs were eliminated. Many high-energy physicists and technicians who worked at the SSC Laboratory were forced to find employment in other fields. Others researchers, however, were hopeful they could use SSC technology at research centers such as the Fermi National Accelerator Laboratory and CERN, the European Laboratory for Particle Research in Geneva, Switzerland.

Programmed for disaster

In retrospect, experts have concluded that, as the most expensive research basic research project in history, the SSC seemed almost programmed for disaster. There were simply too many people who were against the idea of the $11 billion machine. From the outset, the base of support for the SSC was weak, consisting mainly of high-energy physicists and business and government leaders representing companies and states that could directly reap profits from the venture. Most important of all, the American public could not understand why top national priority should be given to an instrument that could solve abstract scientific problems but would have limited use in the real world.

FOR FURTHER REFERENCE

Periodicals

Anderson, Christopher. "The Anatomy of a Defeat." *Science.* October 29, 1993, p. 645.

Glashow, Sheldon L., and Leon M. Lederman, "The SSC: A Machine for the Nineties." *Physics Today.* March 1985, pp. 28–37.

Roush, Wade. "Colliding Forces: Life after the SSC." *Science.* October 28, 1994, pp. 532–34.

Toxic Vapor Leak in Bhopal, India

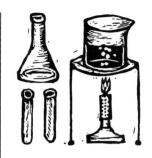

DECEMBER 3, 1984

The Bhopal disaster raised questions not only about the way Union Carbide operated its plant in India, but also about the chemical industry in general.

On the morning of December 3, 1984, a poisonous cloud of methyl isocyanate (MIC) gas escaped from the Union Carbide plant in Bhopal, India, and drifted over the city. (Methyl isocyanate is a highly toxic, or poisonous, compound used in making pesticides.) Thousands of people were killed and many more were badly injured as the gas attacked their nervous systems. Somehow, water had been mixed into the wrong MIC storage tank, causing an increase in pressure that blew open a valve. The ensuing explosion allowed fifty thousand pounds of deadly gas to escape, spreading death and destruction to residents in the Bhopal area. Indian courts eventually ruled that the accident happened as a result of negligence on behalf of Union Carbide, but the company continued to deny responsibility for the toxic release. The disaster has prompted harsh public scrutiny of chemical plants on a worldwide basis.

Large amounts of MCI stored

The Union Carbide site at Bhopal was first developed in 1969 as a mixing and packaging plant for pesticides (chemicals used to kill plants and animals, especially insects) imported from the United States. In 1980 the plant was expanded to manufacture the pesticides Sevin and Temik. One chemical

The Union Carbide plant explosion allowed fifty thousand pounds of deadly methyl isocyanate gas to escape, spreading death and destruction in the Bhopal area.

used in large quantities in the production process was methyl isocyanate (MIC), a highly toxic compound that is also highly explosive. Methyl isocyanate was stored in large 15,000-gallon underground tanks on the Bhopal site. These tanks were more than three times the size of MIC storage containers at any other chemical manufacturing facility.

Toxic vapor is released

For six weeks prior to the day of the accident, the MIC production unit at Bhopal had been temporarily shut down. As is usual during downtime, workers were repairing and cleaning equipment, including filters in the lines that carried MIC from the storage tanks into the processing unit. On the morning of the accident, a worker had closed a valve to prevent water from flowing into MIC tank 610 while he was washing a filter. He forgot, however, to insert a metal disc into the valve to seal it. Two other valves were completely clogged and the remaining

Great Misadventures

two were partially blocked. When this situation became apparent, the filter washing process was halted, then resumed a short time later.

Soon plant operators noticed a sudden rise in pressure in tank 610, from two to thirty to fifty-five pounds per square inch. Leaking water was reacting with MIC to create intense heat. By this time nothing could be done to prevent, or even slow down, a runaway reaction. The operators attempted to activate safety systems, but the systems either were not working, could not handle the vapor pressure load, or would create additional problems if used.

Toxic cloud causes panic and horror

Within ninety minutes approximately twenty-seven tons of MIC vapor and fourteen tons of reaction products were released into the atmosphere. A toxic cloud hovered over fifteen square miles of slums located downwind of the plant. Narrow streets and flimsy dwellings were clogged with human beings and animals frantically gasping for breath. The victims struggled under a heavy white vapor—twice as heavy as air—coming from the plant and filling low-lying areas. The gas was instantly deadly, killing people up to five miles away from the site. The neighborhood where the greatest loss of life occurred was four miles from the plant.

Thousands killed and injured

The Indian Supreme Court's official estimate placed the number of fatalities at 3,000 people, while other investigators reported 2,500 to 5,000 dead. Medical personnel stated that up to 12,000 people died from asphyxiation, suffocation, or exposure to the effects of the toxic vapor. An Indian government commission reported 30,000 people with permanent injuries, 20,000 with temporary injuries, and 150,000 with minor injuries. These figures have been disputed by victims' rights organizations as being much too low.

Injuries from the MIC vapor caused acute respiratory distress, eye irritation, and circulatory, gastrointestinal, and central nervous system disorders. Long-term effects included chronic lesions of the eyes, permanent scarring of the lungs, and injuries to the liver, brain, heart, kidneys, and immune

BHOPAL RAISES CONCERNS
The Bhopal disaster raised questions not only about the way Union Carbide operated its plant in India, but also about the chemical industry in general. People all over the world became concerned about the potential for accidents at other facilities that use MIC. Public-interest groups demanded to be told why Union Carbide was allowed to operate its plant in such an unsafe manner. They also wanted to know how a shantytown could be built around the facility without Union Carbide being required to have an emergency evacuation plan.

system. The yearly rate of spontaneous abortions and infant deaths in Bhopal after the accident was three to four times the regional rate.

Union Carbide scrutinized

The disaster led to an investigation of Union Carbide operations at the Bhopal plant, but the exact cause of the MCI release is still not known. Systems typically used in modern processing plants were either not in place, out of service, or not set properly prior to the explosion. Investigators could only make guesses about what happened.

In addition to finding the unsealed valve and several leaky valves, investigators discovered other factors that contributed to the toxic release. For instance, tank 610 was seventy-five to eighty-seven percent full, well above the fifty to sixty percent recommended in Union Carbide safety standards. Tank 619, which was supposed to be empty as a safety overflow, contained approximately twelve tons of MIC. The MIC in tank 610 was also contaminated by chloroform (a toxic liquid), which reacts both with MIC and with the stainless steel walls of the storage tank. The chloroform level was much higher than that recommended by company safety standards. Finally, the temperature of MIC in tank 610 was between fifteen and twenty degrees Celsius. Standard safe storage procedures specify a temperature of zero to five degrees Celsius, but preferably lower.

Union Carbide charged with negligence

When the investigation was completed, Indian prosecutors brought charges of criminal negligence against Indian and

American managers of Union Carbide. Several months after the accident, Union Carbide claimed that an angry employee had sabotaged the plant by deliberately allowing water to enter the MIC storage tank. However, no one associated with the Bhopal plant has been officially charged with sabotage. After several years of negotiations, Union Carbide reached a settlement with the government of Rajiv Gandhi in 1989. The company agreed to pay $470 million in exchange for the dismissal of all criminal charges against Union Carbide officials.

Legal battle continues

The settlement was challenged on legal grounds, but upheld by the Indian Supreme Court in 1991. Nevertheless, the Indian government of Prime Minister P. V. Narasimha Rao refused to recognize the court's decision, demanding that Union Carbide pay the original claim of $3.3 billion. The government also began pursuing criminal charges against company officials. Union Carbide India was ordered to pay $190 million in interim funds. Under the Bhopal Claims Act, the Indian government is giving survivors two hundred rupees (approximately ten dollars) a month from the fund. These payments are to last as long as the Bhopal case remains unsettled. Legal debate over the Bhopal disaster is expected to continue for several years.

FOR FURTHER REFERENCE

Books

Kurzman, D. *A Killing Wind: Inside Union Carbide and the Bhopal Disaster.* New York City: McGraw-Hill, 1987.

The *Challenger* Explosion

JANUARY 28, 1986

After the *Challenger* explosion, NASA faced an uphill struggle to regain its special status as a federal agency and scientific program.

On January 28, 1986, the National Aeronautics and Space Administration (NASA) launched the space shuttle *Challenger* from Cape Canaveral, Florida. Seventy-three seconds into the flight, however, the shuttle's solid rocket O-rings failed. (The booster rockets were built in sections and then strapped onto the shuttle. The rubber O-rings were required to seal the sections together.) This failure triggered an explosion that destroyed the *Challenger* and killed its crew of seven astronauts.

After the accident, on February 3, 1986, President Ronald Reagan established the Rogers Commission to investigate the catastrophe. The commission found that the O-rings had failed because unusually cold weather before and during the launch caused the rings to stiffen and to lose their seal. The most shocking finding, however, was that NASA administrators knew the O-rings were faulty but had considered the problem an "acceptable risk." After the investigation, the commission recommended that NASA redesign the solid rocket booster joints, improve astronaut escape systems, and reform shuttle program management structure.

The *Challenger* crew walks out to the shuttle before launch on January 28, 1986. ▶ Schoolteacher Christa McAuliffe (second from right) was a specially appointed member of the crew.

How a space shuttle works

A space shuttle is a reusable, airplane-like vehicle which is also called a "winged orbiter." The shuttle is used to transport scientific equipment, such as weather and communications satellites, into space. (A satellite is a vehicle that orbits the Earth, Moon, or other celestial body.) The shuttle is fired by three main engines. Attached to the shuttle are two rocket boosters (which help the engines launch it from the ground) and an external fuel tank (which contains liquid propellant for the engines). The shuttle takes off from a nose-first, vertical position, with the engines and booster rockets resting on the launch pad. At liftoff the vehicle is powered by the engines and the booster rockets. After two minutes the boosters use up their fuel and separate from the shuttle. At the time of separation, parachutes on the boosters are automatically triggered and carry the rockets down to the ocean, where they are recovered.

Eight minutes into the flight, the shuttle's main engines shut down and the external fuel tank is released. The tank burns up as it reenters Earth's atmosphere. With the help of two "Orbiting Maneuvering System" (OMS) engines, the shuttle then enters orbit in space. To return to Earth, the shuttle turns around, reduces speed by firing the OMS engines, and reenters Earth's atmosphere. The shuttle then lands like an airplane.

Regular shuttle flights planned

In 1982, four years before the disastrous *Challenger* mission, a National Security Decision Directive had given the shuttle program the highest national priority. Although the United States was scheduling all of its satellites for shuttle launch by the end of 1985, the nine-billion-dollar program was behind schedule. Nevertheless, 1986 was to be a breakthrough year for the shuttle program. In January 1986, NASA announced that it would launch fifteen missions, using all four of its shuttles—*Columbia, Challenger, Atlantis,* and *Discovery*—during the next twelve months. The year did not get off to a good start, however. After at least seven separate postponements, the first shuttle mission, *Columbia,* was finally launched on January 12. Bad weather prolonged the flight, however, and the spacecraft returned on January 18. NASA's tight 1986 schedule was already in jeopardy.

An inflexible deadline

In the days that followed, everyone worked feverishly to prepare another shuttle, the *Challenger*, for a January mission. *Challenger* had completed its last space mission on November 6, 1985. The ambitious 1986 project involved the much-publicized "Teacher in Space" program. A New Hampshire schoolteacher named Christa McAuliffe had been appointed a member of the crew. Her assignment was to broadcast live satellite reports about space travel to students throughout the world. NASA was also launching a Data-Relay Satellite (TDRS) and the high priority Spartan-Halley comet research observatory. The mission was scheduled to last six days, during which time the Spartan observatory would be recovered from orbit. Because of tight schedule requirements, the Spartan could be orbited no later than January 31. This inflexible deadline led NASA to prepare plans to skip the *Challenger* mission if it could not fly by the end of the month.

Although Spartan project scientists had recommended an afternoon launch, the *Challenger* was ultimately scheduled to lift off in midmorning. Ironically, this shift was due to safety considerations. If the *Challenger* had an engine failure during the launch, the shuttle would glide to an emergency landing site at Casablanca, on the west coast of Africa. NASA argued that an afternoon launch from Florida meant that the emergency landing in Africa would occur at night. This situation would have to be avoided because the Casablanca runway was not equipped with lights.

On January 15, 1986, NASA had held a teleconference Flight Readiness Review for the upcoming *Challenger* mission, linking up the various centers involved with the project. All systems had been reviewed in detail, from the engineering of the spacecraft to the in-flight responsibilities of the Johnson Space Center in Houston, Texas, and the Marshall Space Flight Center in Huntsville, Alabama. The conference had concluded with a "Go for launch" in the midmorning.

Crew experiences delays

The seven-person crew chosen for the mission was commanded by Francis Scobee, who had piloted a 1984 shuttle mission. His pilot, Michael Smith, had never flown in space.

Ellison Onizuka, Ronald McNair, and Judith Resnick, the mission specialists who ran the satellites and experiments, were all experienced space travelers. The payload specialist in charge of the TDRS satellite was Gregory Jarvis, who had no previous space flight experience. As a civilian, McAuliffe also had never traveled in space.

The launch of the *Challenger* was originally set for January 22, 1986, but it was delayed. Additional postponements occurred on January 24 and January 25. Then a forecast of bad weather for the 26th held up the mission until Monday the 27th. On this date, a problem with a hatch bolt developed. By the time the problem was corrected, however, crosswinds had increased to a dangerous thirty knots (nautical miles) per hour. Although the crew was ready to launch and the shuttle had been fueled, liftoff had to be rescheduled yet again for the following day.

Shuttle is launched

During the night of January 27, 1986, the temperature at Cape Canaveral dropped to well below freezing. This prompted a late-night review of the prospects for a successful *Challenger* takeoff by NASA managers and contractors, who were becoming increasingly concerned about the cold weather. In fact, no shuttle had ever been launched at a temperature lower than fifty-three degrees Fahrenheit.

During these discussions, engineers from Morton Thiokol, a NASA contractor, expressed concern that the O-rings on the solid rocket boosters would stiffen in the cold and thereby lose their ability to act as a seal. The engineers apparently were unable to make a fully convincing case, particularly since the O-rings had never been tested at low temperatures. With NASA managers pushing for a decision, Thiokol managers overruled their own engineers and signed a statement claiming that the solid rocket boosters were safe for launch at the colder temperatures.

During the final hours before takeoff January 28, 1986, NASA turned its attention to another problem. During the previous night, when temperatures had ranged between nineteen and twenty-nine degrees Fahrenheit, ice had formed on the shuttle and launchpad. Scientists were concerned about icicles

APOLLO I TRAGEDY The *Challenger* disaster marked the first time American astronauts were lost during a mission in space. At the beginning of the Apollo manned flight program, however, an equally tragic event occurred on the ground. At 1:00 p.m. on January 27, 1967—almost nineteen years to the day before the *Challenger* explosion—astronauts Virgil "Gus" Grissom (1926–1967), Edward White (1930–1967), and Roger Chaffee (1935–1967) entered the *Apollo I* space vehicle. The men began conducting a "plugs-out" test of equipment, which continued routinely throughout the afternoon. At 6:31 p.m., technicians in the control room outside the capsule heard someone say, "There's a fire in here."

It took five minutes to open the hatch to the *Apollo I* capsule. By that time all three astronauts were dead, having been suffocated within a matter of seconds by lethal fumes. (Their space suits, however, had protected the men from being incinerated.) The cause of the fire was determined to be a short circuit near Grissom's seat. The accident delayed the progress of the Apollo program and raised serious questions about the feasibility of spaceflight. The next Apollo missions were unmanned flights that tested the safety of the equipment.

potentially breaking off during launch and damaging the insulating tiles that protected the shuttle as it reentered the Earth's atmosphere. The launch was therefore delayed from 9:38 A.M. to 10:38, and then to 11:38. During this time, inspection teams surveyed the craft's condition and reported no abnormalities due to ice buildup. Finally, at precisely 11:38 A.M. Eastern Standard Time, the *Challenger* launched off from Cape Canaveral to begin its tenth flight into space.

Shuttle explodes

As the *Challenger* rose into a clear, but cold, blue sky, no one on the ground or in the shuttle realized that a tongue of flame was extending from the right-hand booster rocket toward the giant fuel tank. The crowd of spectators, which included McAuliffe's husband and two children, as well as a group of her students, cheered as the shuttle ascended. The vehicle then rolled to align itself on the proper flight path and throttled back its engines. At about fifty-nine seconds into the launch, however, the plume of flame became evident to observers on the ground.

By sixty-four seconds into the launch, a gaping hole had formed in the casing of the booster rocket from which the

flame was escaping. At seventy-two seconds the flame loosened the strut (support) that attached the rocket to the external tank. At that moment, the cockpit's voice recorder captured the only indication that anyone on board was ever warned of any serious trouble: Smith uttered "Uh oh." One second later, the loosened booster rocket slammed into the *Challenger,* detaching its right wing. At an altitude of forty-eight thousand feet, with the shuttle traveling at twice the speed of sound, the rocket then crashed into the fuel tank and set off a massive explosion.

Debris crashes to Earth

To many spectators unfamiliar with shuttle launches, the accident seemed like a spectacular staging (separation) of the booster rockets. But the disaster became apparent when the fireball widened and debris began to scatter. The crowd of spectators—and millions of people watching the event on television—fell silent, spellbound with disbelief. The shuttle itself was no longer visible. Although NASA began rescue operations immediately, the chances of finding survivors were remote. During the stage of a flight when the rocket boosters are thrusting (driving the spacecraft upward with an initial burst of power), the crew has no way of stopping the launch or ejecting from the spacecraft. In fact, there was nothing anyone could do if something went wrong at that critical moment. The *Challenger* exploded twenty miles off the coast of Florida, and the force of the explosion pushed debris to an altitude of twenty miles. For the next hour, burning fragments of the shuttle continued to rain down on recovery teams.

Crew module is examined

Among the worst accidents in the twenty-five-year history of manned spaceflight, the *Challenger* disaster marked the first time American astronauts were lost during a mission. Footage of the explosion, replayed continuously on television, sent shock waves through the nation. A few days after the disaster, President Reagan eulogized (praised) the crew during a nationally televised memorial ceremony at the Johnson Space Center in Houston. On February 3, 1986, Reagan established a Presi-

◄A spectator watches the *Challenger* explode.

dential Commission to investigate the accident, appointing former Secretary of State William B. Rogers as the commission chair. Six weeks after the disaster, the shuttle's crew module was recovered from the Atlantic ocean floor. The *Challenger* crew members were subsequently buried with full honors.

How long did the crew survive?

There was considerable speculation about whether the crew had survived the initial explosion. Evidence gathered by NASA indicated that the crew survived the breakup and separation of the boosters from the orbiter. NASA concluded that they had also begun to take emergency action inside the crew cabin. Whether all seven astronauts remained conscious throughout the two-minute, forty-five-second free-fall into the ocean remains unknown. At least two crew members, however, were breathing from emergency air packs they had activated. The *Challenger* wreckage has never been exhibited publicly, but the cabin was essentially unrecognizable in the photographs that were eventually released. The force of the impact with the surface of the ocean had compressed the sixteen-and-a-half-foot-high cabin into a solid mass half its original size. The module's thick windows were shattered, but there was no evidence of fire.

An "acceptable risk"

Discussions about the fate of the *Challenger* crew continued throughout the public investigations of the disaster. The Rogers Commission, which had been charged with assessing the accident and recommending preventive measures, conducted a three-month study that involved more than six thousand investigators. During public and closed hearings, the commission recorded fifteen thousand pages of testimony and collected one hundred and seventy thousand pages of documents, as well as hundreds of photographs. It also sponsored independent technical studies, evaluated flight records and film evidence, and recovered debris.

On June 6, 1986, the Rogers Commission released its determination that the immediate physical cause of the *Challenger* disaster was "a failure in the joint between the two lower segments of the right Solid Rocket Motor." The report specifically cited "the destruction of the seals that are intended to prevent hot gases from leaking through the joint during the propellant burn." In attributing the disaster to the destruction of these seals, the commission focused on the O-rings.

After checking into the history and performance of this O-ring sealing system, the Rogers Commission was amazed to find that the O-rings had failed regularly, if only partially, on previous shuttle flights. Although both NASA and Thiokol were concerned about weaknesses in the seals, they had chosen not to undertake a time-consuming redesign of the system. Both organizations had come to regard O-ring erosion as an "acceptable risk" because the seal had never completely failed. But when the *Challenger* flew in the dead of winter, the frigid temperatures made the O-rings so brittle that they did not begin to seal the joint. Even before the shuttle had cleared the launch tower, hot gas was already "blowing by" the rings.

The 256-page Rogers Commission report concluded that "the decision to launch the *Challenger* was flawed." Investigators blamed NASA and Thiokol management procedures for not allowing critical information to reach the right people. This assessment was seconded by the U.S. House of Representatives' Committee on Science and Technology, which spent two months conducting its own hearings. The congressional committee determined that although the technical problem had been recognized early enough to prevent the disaster, "meeting flight schedules and cutting cost were given a higher priority than flight safety."

NASA faces uphill battle

The consequences of these public indictments of NASA were grave. Not only was the nation's confidence in NASA shaken, but its own astronaut corps was extremely disturbed. They had never been consulted or even informed about the dangers that the current sealing-system represented. Allowing astronauts and engineers a greater role in approving launches was among the nine recommendations the Rogers Commission made to NASA. The commission's other recommendations included a complete redesign of the solid rocket booster joints, a review of astronaut escape systems, regulation of the scheduling of shuttle flights to assure safety, and a sweeping reform of the shuttle program's management structure.

Following these decisions, several top officials left NASA. A number of experienced astronauts also resigned due to disillusionment with NASA and frustration over the long redesign process that would delay their chances to fly in space. An American shuttle was not launched again until September 29, 1988. NASA eventually built the *Endeavour,* which replaced the *Challenger.* The *Endeavour* took its first flight on May 7, 1992.

FOR FURTHER REFERENCE

Books

McConnell, Malcolm. *Challenger: A Major Malfunction.* New York City: Doubleday, 1987.

Chernobyl Accident in the Ukraine

APRIL 26, 1986

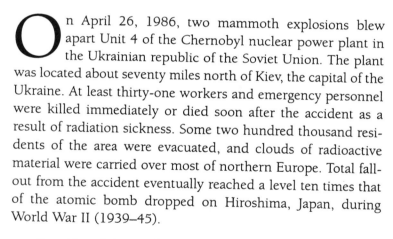

On April 26, 1986, two mammoth explosions blew apart Unit 4 of the Chernobyl nuclear power plant in the Ukrainian republic of the Soviet Union. The plant was located about seventy miles north of Kiev, the capital of the Ukraine. At least thirty-one workers and emergency personnel were killed immediately or died soon after the accident as a result of radiation sickness. Some two hundred thousand residents of the area were evacuated, and clouds of radioactive material were carried over most of northern Europe. Total fallout from the accident eventually reached a level ten times that of the atomic bomb dropped on Hiroshima, Japan, during World War II (1939–45).

Considered the world's worst nuclear power plant disaster, the Chernobyl accident was the result of human error. The key event leading to the disaster was apparently a decision by the plant crew to carry out a controlled experiment. Operators wanted to know what effect a power outage would have on the system. What followed the crew's decision was a series of six major mistakes. After the accident, Soviet officials were reluctant to make changes in reactor design, but they eventually adopted modifications that made their reactors safer.

A decade before the Chernobyl accident, Western scientists began warning Russian leaders about the dangers of RBMK nuclear reactors.

RBMK is an uncommon design

The Chernobyl complex consisted of four reactors constructed between 1977 and 1983. By 1986, the four units—which were known as RBMKs—were operating nearly at capacity and generating four million kilowatts of electricity. The RBMK design was uncommon, and plants of this kind were found almost exclusively in the countries that made up the former Soviet Union. The reactors were built to perform two quite different functions at the same time: generate electricity and produce plutonium for weapons. The decision to build these plants went back to the beginning of the Cold War (a period of nonmilitary hostility primarily between the United States and the Soviet Union) in the 1950s. The Soviet government committed itself to a weapons-development program that would keep it on a par with the United States nuclear arsenal. Thus the dual-purpose RBMKs were built.

Accident occurs

At 1:24 A.M. on Saturday, April 26, Unit 4 of the Chernobyl Nuclear Power Plant was rocked by two enormous explosions. The roof was blown off the plant and radioactive gasses and materials were sent more than thirty-six hundred feet into the atmosphere. Two workers were killed instantly and another dozen received levels of radiation that would cause their deaths within the next two weeks. As with most nuclear accidents on Soviet soil, government officials made no public announcement about the event. The Soviets finally acknowledged the disaster when monitoring instruments in Sweden detected a dramatic increase in wind-borne radiation. The news was reported on April 28 in a short, five-sentence report by Tass (the official Soviet news agency).

The political situation in the Soviet Union in 1986 was not what it had been a decade earlier, when the government exercised total control of information. On May 14, First Secretary Mikhail Gorbachev, acting within his new policy of glasnost (freer dissemination of news and information), went on national television. Gorbachev provided the world with a detailed description of all that was known at the time about the explosions. Still, it would be many months before all the details of the accident were unraveled.

THE SOVIET RBMK
REACTOR The RBMK reactor contains a number of design characteristics that make it risky to operate. A decade before the Chernobyl accident, Western scientists began warning Russian leaders about these dangers. The Soviets, however, continued to have confidence in the RBMK. Not only did it meet both commercial and military needs, but it also—unlike Western reactors—could be refueled without extended downtime.

The most significant problem with the RBMK design, however, was that it did not have a containment shell, a standard feature of all reactors in the United States. The containment shell prevents gases and radioactive materials from being released into the atmosphere during an accident. (The Three Mile Island accident in 1979, for instance, would have been immeasurably more serious without a containment shell.) Another problem with the RBMK is that a loss of cooling water increases the rate of fission (the splitting of the nucleus of an atom), hence more heat is produced in the core. The RBMK was therefore most likely to go out of control when it was operating at lowest power. All of these factors led to the Chernobyl disaster on April 26, 1986.

A controlled experiment

The key event leading to the disaster was apparently a decision by the plant crew to carry out an unauthorized experiment. Operators wanted to know what would happen if there was a power outage and steam stopped flowing to the turbines (engines that spin to produce power). They wondered whether the kinetic energy of the spinning turbine blades would be sufficient to maintain the cooling pumps until the emergency diesel generators turned on. The way to find out, the crew reasoned, was to conduct a controlled test of such a situation. The decision to complete the experiment was followed by a series of six major mistakes made by workers. Any one error by itself would not have been fatal, but the combination of all six was to prove disastrous.

Perhaps the most critical error was the crew's decision to disable the emergency coolant system. At the outset of the test, the reactor began to lose power. Because the test could be continued only if the reactor remained in operation, the crew disabled the coolant system. (The RBMK reactor design meant that the loss of any coolant water would increase its fission rate and therefore its power level.) The reactor continued to lose power, so the crew removed all the control rods from the two thousand-ton graphite block core. (Control rods dampen the nuclear reaction when lowered into the block.)

This move dramatically increased the fission rate of the reactor, which instantly became a cause for concern. As power in the core began to increase, the crew attempted to reinsert the control rods manually. But the channels into which the rods were supposed to fit had deformed because of heat in the core. The rods did not drop properly, and power released in the reactor went out of control. As steam vented from the reactor, water level dropped dramatically in the core. Loss of water, in turn, increased power output from fission reactions. In less than a second, power output from the core increased a hundredfold. As temperatures increased to more than five thousand degrees Celsius, parts of the core melted. Molten (melted) metal reacted with the remaining cooling water, producing hydrogen gas and even more steam. Finally the top of the reactor was blown off—the first of the two explosions.

The second explosion

Details of the second explosion are less clear. Some authorities believe that it was largely a chemical and physical phenomenon, like the first explosion. It would take no more than a few seconds for the hydrogen gas initially produced to be ignited by heat released during the meltdown. Other researchers speculate that the second explosion may have been a pure nuclear reaction. Unlike most reactors in use today, an RBMK can at least theoretically explode like a nuclear (atomic) bomb. Some scientists suggest that parts of the molten core may have achieved critical mass (produced an explosion) during meltdown. If that had occurred, then a true bomb-like explosion could have occurred, accounting for the second explosion.

Soil contaminated

The Chernobyl accident has had both short-term and long-term effects on the local area, on the world as a whole, and on the further development of the nuclear power industry. In addition to the 31 people who died immediately or within two weeks of the accident, another 299 were injured. About 135,000 residents were evacuated from the area within 18

The Chernobyl plant after the explosion. Total fallout from the accident eventually reached a level ten times that of the atomic bomb dropped on Hiroshima, Japan.

miles of the damaged plant, and later another 200,000 were told to leave other areas. These numbers, however, do not begin to reflect the magnitude of the damage inflicted on human health over the next generation and beyond.

Plants and animals in the immediate area of Chernobyl and downwind of the plant were heavily contaminated by fallout (radioactive particles that fall through the atmosphere). Crops could not be harvested and most farm animals were destroyed to prevent their use as food. In the mid-1990s, more than a decade after the accident, levels of radiation were still so high in some areas that no native food could be grown or consumed. People survived on food shipped in from safe areas.

The chief contaminants remaining in the soil are cesium 137 and strontium 90. Since their half-lives are thirty and twenty-eight years, respectively, these contaminants will constitute a hazard for many more decades if they are not removed. (Half-life is the time required for half of the atoms of a radioactive substance to become disintegrated.) Decontamination and removal of contaminated topsoil has not been progressing very rapidly, however. The result is that many residents in the Chernobyl area still face a constant and serious health risk from radioactive particles in the environment.

Fallout spreads to Europe

The fallout that covered the western Soviet Union spread to parts of Europe, causing concern about food supplies across the continent. On May 7, 1986, for example, Canadian customs officials announced that vegetables arriving from Italy were contaminated with radioactive iodine 31. At about the same time, member states of the European Community banned all fresh meat produced in Eastern Europe. As far away as Lapland, reindeer meat was so contaminated with radiation that it was declared unfit for human consumption.

Workers build a sarcophagus

And what of the reactor itself? Soviet engineers used a variety of techniques to put out the flames in the reactor, then to cool it down, and finally to cover up the damaged facility. One of the first steps, for example, was to pump liquid nitrogen into the core to cool it down and to put out fires. Next, thousands of tons of sand, clay, lead, and boron were dumped on top of the plant from helicopters. These materials absorbed neutrons and helped put out fires. In the surrounding area, dikes were built to contain contaminated water, and several inches of soil were removed and transferred to a storage area.

Eventually, workers began to build a huge sarcophagus (tomb) over the damaged plant. The steel-and-concrete shell was designed to isolate the ruins of Unit 4 for the hundreds of years during which the unit would continue to emit dangerously high levels of radiation. The first shell did not last nearly that long, however. By 1992 the shell had cracked and begun to leak radioactive material into the environment. The Ukrainian government found it necessary to make plans for a second shell, stronger than the first, to install on top of the original sarcophagus.

Officials are reluctant to change

After a horrible disaster like the one at Chernobyl, scientists always hope to learn new information that can be used to increase safety in the future. At first, officials of the former Soviet Union were reluctant to consider changes in the design of their RBMK plants. They felt that operator errors, and not plant problems, had caused the accident. Eventually, however, they adopted a number of modifications that would make the reactors safer. (For example, control rods were designed so that they could not be removed completely from the reactor core.)

Scientists outside the Soviet Union, however, did not benefit significantly from events that occurred during the accident. Most non-Soviets had long been leery of the RBMK design and had rejected the use of such plants in their own countries. As one American nuclear expert said, "Most of the lessons from Chernobyl have been learned already and applied in the United States."

Possibly the final legacy of the Chernobyl accident is its impact on worldwide opinion about nuclear power. The impact varied from country to country. In the United States, where memories of the 1979 Three Mile Island accident (see "Science and Technology" entry) had not yet faded, Chernobyl merely confirmed fears about the use of nuclear power. In France, Japan, Belgium, and other nations that depend heavily on nuclear power, the Chernobyl accident had hardly any impact. And in a few nations, such as Great Britain, the accident for the first time opened up a heated debate about the role of nuclear power as a source of energy.

FOR FURTHER REFERENCE

Periodicals

Barringer, F. "Chernobyl: Five Years Later, the Danger Persists." *The New York Times Magazine.* April 14, 1991, p. 28.

Exxon *Valdez* Oil Spill

MARCH 24, 1989

More than fifteen hundred miles of Alaska shoreline were polluted, and many thousands of birds and sea otters were killed by the Exxon *Valdez* oil spill.

In the early morning of March 24, 1989, the tanker Exxon *Valdez* ran aground on Bligh Reef in Alaska, spilling 10.8 million gallons of crude oil into Prince William Sound. More than fifteen hundred miles of shoreline were polluted, and many thousands of birds and sea otters were killed. Although the immediate cause of the grounding was human error, the accident also resulted from negligence on the part of government and industry. The *Valdez* misadventure is a sobering reminder of the extent to which the United States is dependent on oil to fuel a highly technological society.

Spill occurs

The Exxon *Valdez* left the dock at Valdez, Alaska, at 9:12 P.M. on March 23, 1989. The big oil tanker was embarking on a five-day run to Long Beach, California. At the helm was Captain Joseph Hazelwood, who had nineteen years of experience with Exxon Shipping. There had been a report of a heavy flow of Columbia Glacier ice into Prince William Sound, and this ice soon showed up on the ship's radar. A couple of hours into the voyage, the *Valdez* notified the Coast Guard station at Valdez of its intention to leave the lane designated for outbound vessels. In an attempt to avoid the ice, the ship was instead taking the lane designated for inbound vessels.

The *Valdez,* however, went farther out of its way than it had reported. Soon the tanker was headed for Bligh Reef, which lay six miles ahead. Since there appeared to be a gap of only nine-tenths of a mile between the edge of the ice and Bligh Reef, a well-timed turn would be necessary. Before leaving the deck to go below to his cabin, Hazelwood told Third Mate Gregory Cousins to make a right turn when the vessel was across from the light on Busby Island. He also told Cousins to skirt the edge of the ice, but failed to specify an exact course.

Perhaps because Cousins was looking at the radar screen, the tanker slipped past the light without starting to turn. At 12:04 A.M. on March 24, 1989, the Exxon *Valdez* ran up onto Bligh Reef. The accident caused a tear in the bottom of the tanker, and oil was soon spewing into the surrounding waters.

Cleanup is slow and confused

Exxon took responsibility for management and cleanup of the spill. The process was monitored by the Alaska

Exxon *Valdez* captain Joseph Hazelwood had nineteen years of experience as an oil tanker pilot at the time of the accident in Prince William Sound.

Department of Environmental Protection, the U.S. Coast Guard, and special interest groups. In spite of this attention, the response to the spill was slow and confused. Mobilizing the necessary equipment and materials was the first major challenge. It took fourteen hours for the first barge to be loaded with containment booms in Valdez and then travel to the spill. (Containment booms are inflatable objects that float on the water and keep the oil from spreading.) A day and a half into the spill, only a small line of booms was visible from the air. In addition to being too late and too few, there were further problems with the booms. Some sank because of leakage or punctures in their buoyancy compartments. Others intended for use in protected harbors were mistakenly deployed in open seas.

There were some small successes, however. About five days into the spill, when the effort to contain the great mass of the

THE LARGEST SPILL IN AMERICA The Exxon *Valdez* oil spill was widely reported, but there have been many other major spills about which the public has been generally unaware. Between 1978 and 1990, there were nineteen hundred oil spills of more than ten thousand gallons worldwide. Of these, twenty-six were of more than ten million gallons, with the *Valdez* spill falling toward the low end of this group. The Exxon *Valdez* spill became so widely known for two reasons: first, because it was the largest spill in the United States and in North American waters, and second, because it did so much damage in the enclosed waters of Prince William Sound. Oil could not disperse and break down as easily in this area as it could have on the high seas. Before the spill, Prince William Sound—with its snow-capped mountains, many islands, and abundant wildlife—was a place of rare beauty.

spill had failed, the booms were finally used to protect a number of fish hatcheries. Another fairly successful aspect of the cleanup was the lightening operation (the transferral of the remaining oil from the Exxon *Valdez* into another tanker). By early Saturday morning, more than twenty-four hours into the spill, the Exxon *Baton Rouge* had tied up alongside the tanker, and about four-fifths of the cargo of oil was recovered.

Other methods attempted

Other methods were used to keep the oil from spreading. The first method involved chemical dispersants (chemicals used to remove oil from water). Dispersants do not actually remove oil from the water; rather, they break oil into tiny droplets that can have a toxic (poisonous) effect on marine organisms for about six hours. Such chemicals are not often used or are applied with caution. Three days into the spill, the Coast Guard authorized Exxon to apply dispersants. The chemicals, however, did not work. By that time gale-force winds had churned the oil into a mousse (a thick substance), so it could no longer be treated with dispersants. Even if authorization had come earlier, there was not nearly enough dispersant available to treat a spill of this magnitude. By Monday morning, when a blizzard was producing twenty-five-foot waves, less than one percent of the spilled oil had been recovered.

Cleanup crews also used bioremediation, another controversial process that was ultimately futile. Bioremediation involves

Cleanup response to the Exxon *Valdez* oil spill was initially slow and confused. Many different methods—from dispersants to bioremediation—were eventually used, with varied success.

spraying fertilizer onto beaches to stimulate growth of naturally occurring bacteria that degrade (break down) oil and change it to a harmless substance. Only seventy miles of shoreline were treated with this fertilizer, however, because of the uncertain long-term effects of the bacteria on other life forms.

Shoreline cleanup begins

After the failure of efforts to retrieve the remaining spilled oil or at least keep it from spreading, the operation focused on cleaning shorelines. More than eleven thousand people, fourteen thousand vessels, and eighty-five aircraft were involved in the cleanup. The rocks along shorelines were washed with hot absorbent towels. Work crews collected dead animals so that oil would not get into the food chain, and other people brought sick wildlife in for treatment. More than one hundred endangered bald eagles, thirty-six thousand seabirds, and seven thousand sea otters were found dead. (Many more are thought to have died but were never recovered.) Only 627 birds and 200 otters were saved in the rescue effort.

Environmental scientists were skeptical about the value of the cleanup. When Exxon finished the majority of the effort in September 1989, some of the shoreline appeared to be clean. Nevertheless, a layer of tar still existed not far below the shore surface. In some places, the oil had penetrated four feet into the earth and threatened to soak in even more deeply. Scientists estimate that, because of the extent of the damage, many marine, wildlife, and plant species will need five to twenty years to restore themselves.

Trans-Alaska Pipeline—a catastrophe waiting to happen?

As the story of the *Valdez* oil spill unfolded, it became apparent that negligence by Hazelwood and Cousins was not the sole cause of the accident. Environmentalists pointed to the Trans-Alaska Pipeline (also called "TAP")—from which the *Valdez* had loaded the oil—as a catastrophe waiting to happen. In 1970 Alyeska, a consortium (cooperating group) of oil companies that included Exxon, had applied to Congress for a permit to build a pipeline. Tapping into the 9.6 billion barrels of oil underneath the frozen ground on Alaska's North Slope, the pipeline was intended to transport oil eight hundred miles from Prudhoe Bay to Valdez. Construction began in 1974 and was completed in 1977. Two million gallons of oil now travel through the pipeline every day, and seventy to seventy-five tankers leave the port of Valdez every month.

Government and industry promises not kept

Many environmentalists and citizens of Alaska opposed the building of the TAP, fearing that a catastrophic oil spill was inevitable. In response, the federal government and the oil industry made safety promises, many of which were not kept. For example, in the early 1970s the federal government promised to require double bottoms on tankers, and oil industry leaders vowed to equip their ships with this feature as soon as possible. (This was a key factor in subsequent congressional approval of the TAP route.) But when the oil industry encountered hard times in the 1980s, double bottoms on tankers were, for the most part, forgotten.

VALDEZ CREW UNAWARE OF NEW RADAR As a result of Coast Guard cutbacks in the 1980s, fewer people were assigned to the Valdez Coast Guard station. Tankers were therefore watched less closely as they moved in and out of the terminal. The radar at the station was also replaced by a less powerful unit. This meant that tankers could no longer be inspected when they left the terminal and could not be tracked as far as Bligh Reef. Unfortunately, the tanker crews had not been informed about the limits of the new radar. If the old radar had still been in use, the Coast Guard might have been able to warn the Exxon Valdez to turn sooner to avoid Bligh Reef.

When the TAP permit was issued, government and industry officials also guaranteed that ice conditions in Prince William Sound would be carefully monitored. State-of-the-art equipment would be used to minimize the chances of a tanker colliding with an iceberg. This monitoring, however, never occurred.

Safety standards also declined over the years. In 1977 the average tanker going out of Valdez carried about forty crew members. By 1989 the same size tankers had crews of twenty men, who worked twelve-to-fourteen-hour days and were usually exhausted. In the first years of the pipeline, Alyeska had a spill-readiness team that worked around the clock running drills and maintaining equipment. By 1982, when public watchfulness had slackened, team members had been assigned to other duties as well. The team and equipment could therefore not be quickly assembled to respond to a spill.

Government and industry respond to spill

As a result of the catastrophic *Valdez* spill, Congress passed the Oil Pollution Act of 1990. The act requires all oil-carrying vessels operating in United States waters to be equipped with double hulls by the year 2015. A Coast Guard study performed after the spill has shown that a double hull on the *Valdez* could have cut the amount of spilled oil by sixty percent. The petroleum industry also responded by contributing seven million dollars to create the Petroleum Industry Response Organization. Five regional centers for fighting oil spills were established along the coasts of the United States.

Although there is significant evidence that Hazelwood had been drinking alcohol before boarding the *Valdez,* and even during the voyage, a jury acquitted him of all charges except the negligent discharge of oil. Nevertheless, the Alaska state legislature acted to require all tanker captains leaving port to take a breath alcohol test no more than one hour before boarding. In addition, tankers now must keep two pilots on the bridge until after they have passed Bligh Reef. Tankers must also be accompanied by two tugboats while still in Prince William Sound, and pilots are no longer allowed to change lanes.

Exxon required to pay

Several lawsuits followed the cleanup efforts. The state of Alaska sued Exxon, but the company countersued. Exxon claimed the state should pay much of the cleanup cost because it had interfered with the use of dispersants. The most significant settlement required that Exxon set up a $900 million dollar fund to pay for damages caused by the spill.

FOR FURTHER REFERENCE

Books

Davidson, Art. *In the Wake of the Exxon* Valdez: *The Devastating Impact of the Alaska Oil Spill.* San Francisco, CA: Sierra Club Books, 1990.

The "Year 2000" Computer Problem

BEGINNING IN 1990s

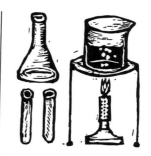

A computer programming decision created a problem of great magnitude.

In the early 1990s, analysts began discussing the potential impact of a largely unanticipated computer crisis. At the root of this crisis was a seemingly minor error: When early computers were designed, programmers designated dates in a six-digit configuration. Two digits were allotted for each of three numbers in a date—month, day, and year. For example, January 1, 1999, was expressed as "01–01–99." The date configuration for January 1, 2000, however, would read "01–01–00." Most computer software and hardware programs would then register "00" the year as "1900," not 2000. Accurate dates are essential to the running of systems and the storage and application of information. When a computer program registers the wrong year (thus the wrong date), systems can malfunction, give inaccurate information, or simply shut down. Programmers have the ability to fix the date problem, but the time and money involved pose a very real dilemma for both businesses and individual users.

The Millennium Bug

The end-of-the-century computer crisis has been called many things, including the "Millennium Bug." Many analysts dispute the use of the word "bug," however, because it suggests a virus (an error deliberately or accidentally introduced into a

345

INCREASING AWARENESS

When computer expert Peter de Jager first published an article called "Doomsday 2000" in a magazine in 1993, no one really knew—or cared—about the "Year 2000 problem" (also known as the "Y2K problem"). When de Jager and coauthor Richard Bergeron wrote *Managing 00:*

Surviving the Year 2000 Computing Crisis four years later, however, people began to take notice. In their book, the authors explain why computers will think that "00" means the year 1900, not 2000. They also offer a variety of ways to deal with the problem on both a business and personal level.

software or hardware program that causes the program to fail). The analysts argue that the problem was not caused by a virus, but instead resulted from negligence and a lack of foresight on the part of computer programmers. Therefore, the names most commonly given to the phenomenon are the "Year 2000 problem" or the "Y2K problem" ("Y" stands for year and "K" stands for 1000).

Worst-case scenarios

One of the common misconceptions is that only personal computers will be affected by the Y2K problem. The reality is that there are computer chips in almost every product, including cars, microwave ovens, videocassette recorders (VCRs), and even airplanes. Imagine flying in a commercial airliner when the clock turns to 12:01 A.M. on January 1, 2000. As the plane is about to land, the landing gear fails to go down. The landing gear, however, is not broken. Instead, the plane's computer has shut the system down because it thinks the year is 1900. This scenario might sound ridiculous, but it could happen. Maintenance records for most planes are stored on computers. Airplanes that are not periodically maintained are automatically grounded. Therefore, if a plane's computer believes that the year is 1900, then the entire maintenance record does not exist and the plane is shut down.

Other potential disasters

There are many other worst-case scenarios that could play out if the Y2K problem persists. For instance, a food shortage could result if grocery stores mistakenly throw away food that—

based on computer-generated tags—has passed its expiration date. Hospitals could be affected as well. Noncompliant computers could instruct hospital staffers to mistakenly discard drugs that actually have correct expiration dates. Life-support systems, such as kidney dialysis machines, could malfunction.

The Y2K problem could also cause economic headaches. Computers that have not been fixed could attach extra interest rates onto loans, forcing many people to default (become unable to pay). Credit-card verification systems may misinterpret expiration date information, and automatic teller machines could shut down. The stock market could even crash if worried investors stop doing business. Other serious situations that could arise from the Y2K problem include drivers' licenses expiring prematurely, elevators getting stuck, security systems failing, and voter registration records becoming invalid.

Archiving nightmare

Another Y2K-related potential problem exists for corporations and institutions, such as libraries and government agencies, that rely on electronic archiving (storing information and data on disks). The archiving issue goes back to the advent of the computer and its promise of a "paperless society." Computer promoters advocated eliminating the need for paper and shelf space—thus cutting costs—by transmitting records and documents electronically, then saving them on disk.

The only trouble is that computers and software programs are constantly changing, and can even become outdated within a year or two. Consequently, records and documents saved on disk a few years earlier can often not be read by newer systems and programs. Aside from stressing the value of keeping old computers, software, and accessories, experts have offered a few suggestions for preserving electronic archives. Ironically, their main recommendation is to print out and save a paper copy whenever possible.

Problems have also beset video game developers. For instance, Jaron Lanier, a pioneer in virtual reality research, was recently asked to display the video game *Moondust*, which he designed in 1982. (Virtual reality programs help make people feel as if they are really part of the computerized action taking place.) In order to do so, Lanier first had to find the exact ver-

EXPERTS PESSIMISTIC The D.C. Year 2000 Group is an informal organization of about 200 people who are working on the Year 2000 problem for government agencies and private industry. Each month the group members meet in Washington, D.C., to discuss their findings. In April 1998 the group conducted a survey of 229 experts to determine the seriousness of the impending Y2K crisis. The results, which were published in *Newsweek* magazine, offered a pessimistic outlook. Eighty-four percent of the experts predicted such problems as a drop in the stock market, bankruptcies, business failures, shortages in fuel, electrical power outages, social disruptions, political crises, and air-traffic-control failures. Most group members were dissatisfied with the efforts of the U.S. government in preparing for Y2K, giving it an overall grade of D–. The departments of defense and transportation both received an F.

sion of the Commodore 64 computer—along with a compatible joystick (a hand-held device for operating the game) and video program—that he used when he originally created the game.

Looking on the bright side

Luckily, there is a solution to the Y2K problem. Older computers and computer chips simply need to be reprogrammed. These devices were originally programmed to display and read dates in a six-digit configuration with the last two spaces representing the year (for example, 1998 would read "98"). In the six-figure model, the year 2000 would be represented by "00," which essentially means "1900" to most computers. Updated computers will display dates in an eight-digit configuration, with four spaces for the year. For example, January 1, 2000, would read "01–01–2000."

One of the positive aspects of the Y2K problem is that it has created many new jobs. People with the skills necessary to reprogram computers—data recovery consultants, testing consultants, and planning consultants—are in high demand. Web site developers, who provide updated information about the Y2K problem for personal users, programmers, and businesses, are also very necessary.

Solutions are expensive

The solution to the Y2K problem is nevertheless quite expensive. The cost to businesses for reconfiguration is between fifty cents and two dollars per computer line. This does not seem like much money at first, but it adds up to millions, even billions, of dollars for an entire project. Large corporations such as Chase Manhattan Bank, for example, plan to spend up to $250 million to prepare for year 2000. The U.S. government expects to spend $30 billion to reprogram its computers. The high cost of the Y2K fix has forced some institutions to seek out other options. For instance, the University of Chicago Hospital has decided to replace its noncompliant system rather than try to fix the old one.

Some companies and institutions may not be able to afford the Y2K correction or may wait too long to administer it. One of the most important institutions lagging behind is the healthcare industry. The main problem is that most hospitals and other healthcare providers cannot afford the reprogramming costs. The insurance industry is also having a hard time finding money to fix its computers. Not surprisingly, among the hardest hit by the Y2K problem is the software industry. While newer software programs and systems have taken Y2K into account, older programs running on older machines will have difficulty functioning.

A high-level response

The Y2K problem is so widespread that U.S. president Bill Clinton has intervened. Because many institutions and corporations are taking a long time to make their computers compliant, Clinton has set up the Council on the Year 2000 Conversion. This group's goal is to help speed up the process. The Securities and Exchange Commission (SEC) has become involved as well. The SEC is requiring businesses to inform the agency of plans to upgrade their computers. Similarly, governments all over the world are forming commissions and developing guidelines in preparation for year 2000. This high-level response shows how important the computer has become in society.

Negligence and lack of foresight

Many observers argue that it is not fair to say that, if people depended less heavily on computers, the impending crisis might not seem so serious. The real problem, they argue, is that early computer developers were short-sighted, even negligent, in designing software and hardware programs. Critics are still puzzling over the fact that as recently as the 1970s and 1980s, software designers did not take into account the Y2K issue. They also say that consumers cannot be faulted for making the computer a necessary part of everyday life and work. There is nothing wrong, they point out, with wanting more convenience and faster progress—both of which the computer has provided.

FOR FURTHER REFERENCE

Periodicals

Jager, Peter de. "Doomsday 2000." *Computerworld.* September 6, 1993.

Levy, Steven. "Will the Bug Bite the Bull?" *Newsweek.* May 4, 1998, p. 62.

The Ban on Silicone Breast Implants

1992

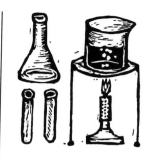

The FDA banned the use of silicone in breast implants until more conclusive test results were available.

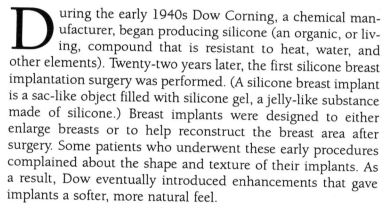

During the early 1940s Dow Corning, a chemical manufacturer, began producing silicone (an organic, or living, compound that is resistant to heat, water, and other elements). Twenty-two years later, the first silicone breast implantation surgery was performed. (A silicone breast implant is a sac-like object filled with silicone gel, a jelly-like substance made of silicone.) Breast implants were designed to either enlarge breasts or to help reconstruct the breast area after surgery. Some patients who underwent these early procedures complained about the shape and texture of their implants. As a result, Dow eventually introduced enhancements that gave implants a softer, more natural feel.

By 1976, however, silicone breast implants had come under Food and Drug Administration (FDA) scrutiny. The following year, the first of many lawsuits was brought against Dow and other companies that manufactured implants. Over the next decade, hundreds of suits were filed by women who said the implants endangered their health. From 1988 to 1991 the FDA required implant manufacturers to provide data supporting the safety of their product. After receiving inconclusive information, the FDA banned silicone implants in 1992. Since the ban, millions of dollars have been awarded to women claiming that their poor health—from muscular disease to chronic illness—resulted from implant use. The con-

A silicone breast implant. Breast implants were designed to either enlarge breasts or to help reconstruct the breast area after surgery.

troversy over silicone implants has prompted many researchers to look for alternative implant substances.

What is silicone?

Two of the "backbones" of silicone are silicon and oxygen. Silicon (a nonmetallic chemical element found abundantly in nature) was first isolated in the 1820s. In the 1880s it was combined with other elements to form useful compounds, including silicone. It was not until the 1940s, however, that E.G. Rochow, a scientific researcher for the General Electric Company, discovered an easy way to form silicone by combining methyl chloride gas (a combination of methane and chlorine) with heated silicon and copper.

Silicone was used extensively during World War II (1939–45) to make waterproof electronic parts such as gaskets for searchlights and superchargers for aircraft engines. The substance also made possible such medical advances as artificial joints, eye lenses, and the Norplant contraceptive (a device implanted under the skin of a woman's arm that slowly releases an artificial hormone that prevents pregnancy).

The first breast implants

Silicone was first used in breast implants during the early 1960s. In addition to giving women the option of improving their appearance, the implants enabled surgeons to reconstruct breasts that had been removed during cancer surgery. In a twenty-five-year period, about one million women had breast implant surgery. Over time, some of these women experienced problems or complications. These problems included localized (limited to a specific area) silicone leakage and hardening of the breast due to tightness of scar tissue (tissue formed from a surgical incision) surrounding the implant. In fact, shortly after the FDA began to review breast implants in the mid-1970s, the first successful lawsuit was won by a woman who was awarded $170,000 for ruptured (broken) implants.

In the 1980s, medical researchers began to suspect that silicone was responsible for other health problems, particularly connective tissue diseases such as rheumatoid arthritis (a degenerative disease of the joints). In 1984, a woman won the first case alleging an implant-related disease. By 1988 the FDA was requiring manufacturers to prove the safety of implants. In part due to media coverage in the early 1990s, many women became concerned about their implants. The FDA began conducting further investigations.

FDA bans implants

In April 1991, the FDA issued a regulation requiring all manufacturers of silicone gel-filled breast implants to submit scientific data proving that their products were safe enough to be on the market. All major manufacturers responded by the July deadline. After reviewing the preliminary findings, the FDA reviewed four of the manufacturers. Three companies were found to have deficiencies in their product safety and effectiveness procedures. The businesses were given the following options: they could take their products off the market, appeal the FDA decision, or conduct their own scientific tests. Eventually, the FDA found many manufacturers had not done proper scientific testing of possible long-term implant effects. As a result, the FDA banned the use of silicone implants in 1992 until more conclusive test results were available.

Dow Corning declares bankruptcy

Some women—both individually and as part of class-action (large group) suits—proceeded to launch a series of legal actions against implant manufacturers. Most of the suits were brought against Dow Corning, the manufacturer of over half the silicone breast implants in use. From 1984 onward, eighteen judgments yielded twenty-five million dollars and numerous out-of-court settlements for plaintiffs (the people who initiated the lawsuits). In 1994, in order to put the lawsuits behind them, the manufacturers offered to pay $4.25 billion to women suffering from ailments believed to be linked to implants. (This was the largest class-action settlement to date.) For various reasons, the suit fell

---

CHARLOTTE MAHLUM'S
STORY When Charlotte Mahlum was thirty-six years old, she had a double mastectomy (both breasts were surgically removed) to prevent breast cancer. Silicone implants were used to reconstruct her breasts. Doctors assured Mahlum that the implants would last a lifetime, and after five years, she was still pleased with her appearance. In 1990, however, Mahlum began to experience joint pain, fatigue, and a tingling sensation in her chest. The implants were removed after a magnetic resonance imaging (MRI) test showed that one implant was releasing silicone into her body. The procedure did not, however, bring an end to Mahlum's ailments.

Over time, Mahlum developed rashes, parched eyes, and terrible headaches. She suffered humiliating episodes of incontinence (lack of bladder control), and her hair fell out. Mahlum sued Dow Chemical, the parent company of Dow Corning, and won. On October 28, 1995, a Nevada jury awarded her $14 million in damages. Even though scientific data did not conclusively link the implants to the ailments suffered by Mahlum, her attorney argued that the studies were flawed. He also argued that Dow Chemical had covered up information about the harmful effects of silicone implants. Ultimately, it seemed, Mahlum's visibly failing health was enough for the jury to decide in her favor.

---

apart and Dow Corning filed for bankruptcy (the company legally claimed it was unable to pay its debts). In 1995, however, the company was still facing over 19,000 lawsuits.

Studies inconclusive

In an effort to bounce back, Dow Coming submitted a reorganization plan to the court. The plan stated that no patient could collect a settlement unless a "science trial" (a court trial based on scientific evidence) concluded that an ailment was caused by an implant. In other words, if the jury in a science trial found silicone implants to be safe, Dow would not have to make any payment to the plaintiffs. The company also offered $2.4 billion to be divided among over 200,000 women who had filed claims. Scientific data regarding the side effects of silicone implants was still not definitive. As a result, by the mid-1990s court decisions based on science tended to favor manufacturers. The successful lawsuits (or trials where the plaintiffs won) were largely based on the theory that manufacturers covered up information that showed the risks of silicone. No direct link had yet been found, however, between silicone and specific health problems.

Companies found guilty

In the late 1990s women were still winning suits against manufacturers of silicone breast implants. For instance, the first round of lawsuits against Dow Corning ended in August 1997. The company was found guilty of concealing information about the health risks of silicone in breast implants. Dow was also found guilty of not properly testing the silicone before it was used in implants. The next phase of the trial involved a class-action suit filed by eight women representing 1,800 women who claimed to have been injured by breast implants. Lawsuits were also filed and won in Canada. In 1995, for instance, Bristol-Myers Squibb agreed to give a $28 million settlement to 4,500 women from Quebec and Ontario who had received implants made by the company. In 1998 Dow Corning announced a $3.2 billion, sixteen-year implant settlement. People with claims had several months to review Dow's proposal and accept or reject it. Claimants who rejected it could sue the company individually.

The women received payment on the basis of the severity of their health problems; a reserve fund was also established for women who might suffer complications in the future. The legal controversy continued into the late 1990s, when a staggering number of lawsuits involving silicone breast implants still waited to be tried in the courts. It is not possible to estimate exactly how much money has been paid out, however, since many cases were settled out of court.

Recent FDA findings

By 1998 the FDA had made definite findings about implants. For instance, research revealed that implants ruptured at a rate of sixty-three percent in women who had them from one to twenty-five years. After twenty-five years, ninety-five percent of women with two silicone breast implants could expect both implants to rupture. The FDA also found that such health problems as connective tissue disease could occur when silicone leaked into the body. The FDA continued to place restrictions on silicone breast implants and guaranteed an ongoing study of the effects. Breast implants are still available, but most are now filled with saline (salt) solution.

FOR FURTHER REFERENCE

Periodicals

Begely, Sharon. "The Trials of Silicone." *Newsweek.* December 16, 1996.

Edwards, Tamala M. "Sleights of Silicone: The Legal Wrangling over Breast Implants May Test the Ability of Science to Stand Up in Court." *Time.* September 1, 1997.

Mad Cow Disease Outbreak

1996

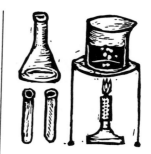

In 1996 the British government caused an international crisis when the Secretary of State for Health announced that ten people had died after eating meat from cattle infected with mad cow disease (technically known as bovine spongiform encephalopathy, or BSE). This announcement contradicted information British officials had been giving to the public for over a decade. After a BSE scare in the late 1980s, researchers and government officials had assured consumers that BSE infection was restricted to cattle and posed no health threat to humans.

The response to news of human exposure was immediate: Consumers refused to buy beef, and British trading partners suspended imports (shipment of goods from one country into another) of British beef products. The beef industry was devastated after the government ordered the slaughter of thousands of diseased cattle. Farmers suffered severe financial losses, even though the government paid out large financial settlements. By 1998 the disease seemed to be disappearing, but serious questions continued to linger about the long-range effects of BSE. The mad cow disaster stands as an example of what can happen when economic interests are placed before concerns about human health.

> The "mad cow" outbreak is an example of what can happen when economic interests are given priority over concerns about human health.

BSE identified

Mad cow disease had been familiar to British livestock farmers (people who raise animals to be butchered for food) and scientists for over a decade. When the condition surfaced in the mid-1980s, veterinarians (medical doctors who treat animals) sought an explanation, at first linking it to other livestock afflictions such as scrapie (a neurological disease in sheep). The condition resisted known treatments, however, and farmers became desperate as hundreds of cattle died. Eventually the disease was identified as BSE, a condition that turns the cow's brain spongy and attacks the central nervous system. As the brain deteriorates, the animal begins to stagger, then collapses and finally dies.

The affliction came to be called "mad cow disease" because of the strange behavior of the stricken animals. Concerns arose about possible threats to human health, but scientists assumed BSE was limited to cattle. Consequently, in the late 1980s the British government assured consumers that they could not be harmed by eating beef, which is a mainstay in the British diet and a huge national industry.

In 1990 the international scientific community was electrified by reports that BSE could be transmitted to other species (forms of life). The disease was found in certain types of antelopes closely related to cattle, such as elands, gemsboks, kudus, nyalas, and oryxes. Even more significantly, mad cow disease was also discovered in domestic cats, which are carnivores (species that eat meat) not directly related to cattle. Eventually BSE was linked to other neurological (nervous system) disorders. Suspicions about a connection between mad cow disease and scrapie were also confirmed. But at this point scientists remained confident that BSE afflicted only animals, not humans. After all, scrapie had been present in British sheep for over 200 years and had never been transmitted to humans. Therefore, researchers reasoned, mad cow disease would behave like scrapie and remain confined to livestock.

Disease found in humans

Then a startling revelation forever changed scientific thinking about BSE. By the early 1990s mad cow disease had been

◀ BSE-infected English cattle are herded into a truck at the St. Austell market for delivery to a slaughterhouse.

CANNIBALS DIE FROM KURU

A study conducted by D. Carleton Gajdusek, an American pediatrician, led to the discovery that mad cow disease (technically called bovine spongiform encephalopathy, or BSE) can be transmitted to humans. During the late 1950s and early 1960s Gajdusek studied a fatal condition called kuru that afflicted the Fore, a cannibal tribe (humans who eat other humans) in New Guinea (an island in the Pacific Ocean). At first he was stumped by the symptoms: Victims of the condition —mostly women in all of the Fore villages—began to shake and lose control of their movements, then they collapsed and finally died.

After exhaustive experimentation and research Gajdusek determined that the Fore had contracted a spongy brain tissue (spongiform encephalopathic) disease during cannibal feasts as early as the 1940s. The condition was then transmitted throughout the tribe during subsequent feasts, which the Fore regarded as important rituals. Gajdusek received a Nobel Prize for his work on kuru in 1976. Gajdusek's findings eventually helped to establish a direct connection between kuru and scrapie (a neurological disease in sheep), Creutzfeldt-Jakob disease (a nervous-system disease in humans), and finally BSE.

linked to another deadly neurological disease caused by spongy brain tissue that had been found in humans three decades earlier. Called kuru, the disease was discovered by American pediatrician (a doctor who treats childhood diseases) D. Carleton Gajdusek (1923–). Kuru was eventually linked to Creutzfeldt-Jakob disease (CJD), a human brain disorder named for neurologists Hans Gerhard Creutzfeldt and Alfons Jakob, who conducted their work from 1913 to 1921. Although CJD was rare, cases had been documented throughout the world.

The last piece of the puzzle was put in place in 1993 when an article appeared in the *Lancet*, the official publication of the British medical association. The journal reported that a farmer who died from CJD may have gotten it from his cattle, which were infected with mad cow disease. Scientists began to speculate about possible BSE connections to other unexplained human deaths in Britain. They concluded that BSE could be causing a new form of CJD.

Threats to humans downplayed

As researchers moved nearer to links between BSE and human neurological diseases, reports of their findings began appearing in newspapers around the world. By 1990 the governments of Australia, the United States, and several European countries had banned the importing of British cattle. British officials were faced with a dilemma: The possible link between BSE and human diseases was indeed disturbing, yet the beef industry was the source of enormous revenues and the national economy would be hurt by a ban. Bowing to pressure from cattle breeders, meat processors, and the food industry, the government issued assurances that the beef was safe for human consumption. The bans were then quickly lifted. But British citizens were worried, especially about eating hamburgers sold at fast-food restaurants. The government, however, shrugged off the public's fears. In 1990 the British public was treated to the spectacle of British Minister of Agriculture John Gummer feeding his four-year-old daughter a hamburger on national television. Similarly journalists downplayed the BSE danger to humans, and humorists had great fun making jokes about crazy cows.

A McDonald's restaurant in London advertises that it does not use British beef products. The restaurant chain stopped using English beef after reports about the "mad cow" outbreak were made public.

EU bans British beef

Nevertheless, the mad cow epidemic continued to spread, and by 1996 over 168,000 diseased cattle were reported in the United Kingdom. The Spongiform Encephalopathy Advisory Committee (SEAC), composed of scientists and physicians, was formed to advise the government on how to handle the crisis. The dramatic climax came in March 1996, when the British Secretary of State for Health, Stephen Dorrell, revealed that ten people had died of CJD as a result of eating meat from BSE-infected cattle.

The news made headlines all over the world. In Britain, beef was banned from school cafeterias, and consumers refused to buy beef from supermarkets. (Ironically, however, people grabbed the meat out of store coolers when the prices were slashed by fifty percent.) The European Union (EU; an economic alliance of several European countries) banned the

OPRAH'S "VEGGIE LIBEL" SUIT

On April 16, 1996, American television talk show host Oprah Winfrey (1954–) interviewed vegetarian activist Howard Lyman on her nationally broadcast program. During the conversation, Lyman revealed that cattle in the United States were being fed ground-up cow parts in their feed. He warned that this practice could spread mad cow disease to humans who consume beef products. A stunned Winfrey vowed she would never eat a hamburger again.

Shortly afterward a group of Texas cattle ranchers sued Winfrey, Lyman, and Winfrey's television production company for $11 million. Claiming that mad cow disease cannot be passed from cattle to humans, the ranchers charged that Winfrey's comment caused a sharp decline in the beef market and a loss of millions of dollars. (The mixing of cattle parts in livestock feed was outlawed in the United States in 1997.) The case went to court, where it was filed under a Texas food defamation law—popularly known as the "veggie libel" law—that forbids making false or derogatory statements about agricultural products. A federal judge threw out those charges, but the trial proceeded on the basis of libel by Winfrey and the others against the beef industry. (Libel is the making of false or unjustified statements that cause a person or group of people to suffer public humiliation.) In March 1998, after two days of deliberation, a jury in Amarillo, Texas, declared that Winfrey and her co-defendants were not guilty. The jubilant television star proclaimed, "Free speech not only lives, it rocks!"

import of British beef as well items that contained gelatin and tallow, which are beef by-products, such as candies, cookies, lipstick, and cough medicines. The McDonald's restaurant chain refused to serve British beef.

After the revelation of BSE-related human deaths, the British government ordered the slaughter of 257,000 cattle over thirty months of age. Herds were also cleared of 127,000 younger animals that appeared to be infected. Then the SEAC reported that lamb and mutton (meat from sheep) might also be contaminated by BSE. The theory was that lambs and sheep had contracted the disease by eating meat-and-bone meal made from the remains of BSE-infected cattle. Within four months deer and goats were added to the list of affected animals.

By this time new cases of BSE in humans had been found in Britain and France, bringing the total number to eighteen. Several instances of BSE in animals had also been discovered in the United States, in spite of strict U.S. government efforts to keep British cattle and beef by-products out of the country. But in September 1996, as the British economy was suffering from

Vegetarians dressed as cows campaign against the consumption of meat outside the Ministry of Agriculture, Fisheries, and Food in London, England.

the EU bans, the government ended the slaughter of cattle. Officials cited "scientific evidence" that indicated the BSE threat had passed or would at least die out by 2000 or 2001.

Entire world infected with BSE?

In 1997 science writer Richard Rhodes published *Deadly Feasts,* a book about BSE, which he calls "the new plague." According to Rhodes, the British government was covering up the true facts about the mad cow epidemic in order to protect the beef industry. Through interviews with scientists, Rhodes determined that the BSE infection was not dying out, and that animals were probably still becoming infected and entering the human food supply.

Rhodes quotes Gajdusek, who found the link between kuru and BSE, as predicting that all animals—chickens, cows, beef cattle, pigs—could be carrying BSE. Gajdusek expressed particular concern about pigs. "Probably all the pigs in England are infected," he told Rhodes. "And that means not only pork. It means your pigskin wallet. It means catgut surgical suture [thread used by surgeons to close incisions], because that's made of pig tissue." Gadjusek warned that blood used in transfusions (injection of blood from one human into another) could also transmit the disease. He pointed out that chickens are susceptible to BSE because they are fed meat-and-bone meal. In turn, vegetables can be infested with BSE since gardens are fertilized with chicken manure. Even people who grow roses could pick up BSE by inhaling dust from the bone meal contained in rose food. Gadjusek was especially worried about dairy products, noting that BSE is probably in butter and milk, which had not yet been investigated.

FOR FURTHER REFERENCE

Books

Rhodes, Richard. *Deadly Feasts: Tracking the Secrets of a Terrifying New Plague.* New York City: Simon & Schuster, 1997.

Periodicals

"Judge Rules in Oprah's Favor in Cattlemen's Suit." *Jet.* March 16, 1998, p. 4.

The Death of Dr. Karen Wetterhahn

1997

O n June 8, 1997, Dartmouth College chemistry professor Karen Wetterhahn died of mercury poisoning. Eleven months earlier, in August 1996, Wetterhahn had been experimenting with dimethyl mercury when she spilled a tiny amount of the dangerous chemical on her hands. Since the latex gloves she was wearing were not adequate protection, the mercury seeped into her skin. The accident—especially the circumstances under which it occurred—sparked a national debate about the risks involved in chemical research.

Tries to help environment

Wetterhahn was conducting an experiment to help the environment when the accident happened. Her objective was to determine the effect that heavy metals (which include mercury, chromium, lead, and arsenic) have on living things. Heavy metals are dangerous to the environment when they accumulate in areas of human activity. These substances can interfere with biological processes such as the transfer of genetic information and metabolism (the chemical changes in a living cell). When heavy metals pollute the environment, victims of contamination often suffer from cancer, circulatory disease, and other disorders.

In a tragic irony, a scientist died as a result of her efforts to help improve the environment.

AN IMPRESSIVE CAREER

Karen E. Wetterhahn (1948–1997) was born in Plattsburgh, New York. In 1970 she graduated magna cum laude (with high honors) from St. Lawrence University in Canton, New York. Five years later she received a doctorate degree from Columbia University in New York City, where she won the Hammett Award in Chemistry. In 1976 Wetterhahn joined the faculty of Dartmouth College in Hanover, New Hampshire. At Dartmouth she initiated a curriculum in structural biology (a field of science that studies biologically active molecules such as DNA, RNA, and proteins).

Wetterhahn also co-founded the Women in Science Project in order to increase the number of women participating in science studies. Throughout her impressive career, she was the author of more than eighty-five research papers and a member of several scientific societies. She was also an Alfred P. Sloan Fellow from 1981 to 1985. Wetterhahn was conducting environmental research when she was accidentally poisoned by a tiny amount of mercury. She died eleven months later. Wetterhahn is survived by her husband and two children.

Uses most toxic compound

In order to carry out the experiment, Wetterhahn used a method called nuclear magnetic resonance (NMR) spectroscopy (the use of an instrument called a spectroscope to form and examine the visible region of the electromagnetic spectrum). With this method, she could examine the binding of mercury to a protein that is involved in the repair of DNA. (DNA, or deoxyribonucleic acid, is a substance present in the nucleus of every cell that determines individual characteristics). Using NMR spectroscopy, Wetterhahn measured the resonance (alternation of a chemical species) of the bound mercury nuclei (plural for nucleus, the center of a cell) to determine what part of the protein was being attacked.

After measuring the resonance, Wetterhahn compared it to a standard compound that contains the element. As the standard (basis) for her comparison Wetterhahn chose the compound known as dimethyl mercury. (Dimethyl is derived from a colorless and highly flammable substance called methane; mercury is a silver-white, heavy metallic element in liquid form.) Dimethyl mercury belongs to the methylmercury group of compounds, which is the most toxic (poisonous) form. It crosses the blood-brain barrier (seeps from the bloodstream into brain tissues) and causes fatal damage to the central ner-

Chemistry professor Karen Wetterhahn (pictured here in her laboratory at Dartmouth College) died on June 8, 1997, from complications of mercury poisoning. Wetterhahn was exposed to the chemical while completing a series of heavy-metal experiments.

vous system and the brain. Symptoms of mercury poisoning include loss of motor (movement) control, numbness in the arms and legs, blindness, and the inability to speak.

Suffers mercury poisoning

In August 1996, Wetterhahn was transferring some dimethyl mercury to an NMR tube when she spilled a tiny amount of the toxic compound on her hands. Even though she was wearing latex gloves, the clear liquid permeated the thin gloves and seeped into her skin within seconds. Wetterhahn did not begin to feel the effects of the exposure until six months later, in January. She then began losing her balance, slurring her speech, and suffering vision and hearing loss. Tests revealed that there was more than eighty times the lethal dose of mercury in her system. Wetterhahn died of mercury poisoning on June 8, 1997, less than a year after the accident.

Mercury poisoning

Scientists have long known that mercury is highly poisonous, but the most significant research on the subject was not done until the mid-twentieth century. Mercury was known to the ancient Chinese, Hindus, and Egyptians. It was used as a medicine by the sixteenth-century German alchemist and physician Paracelsus (Phillipus Bombast von Hohenheim; 1493–1541). Two hundred years later French chemist Antoine-Laurent Lavoisier (1743–1794) recognized mercury as an element (a substance composed of atoms that all have the same number of protons, or positively charged particles, in their nuclei).

During the nineteenth century mercury was used in the manufacture of felt hats, and the phrase "mad as a hatter" was applied to workers who suffered from prolonged contact with the element. Since mercury is not easily discharged from the body, poisoning (known as "mercurialism") takes place slowly. Symptoms include skin conditions, bleeding gums, trembling hands, digestive disorders, kidney ailments, liver disease, and deafness.

Mercury is also a serious threat to the environment, causing the pollution of rivers, lakes, and oceans. Scientists have found that heavy mercury concentrations can contaminate fish and other sea life that are used for food. As a result, ninety-nine countries banned the ocean dumping of mercury and other polluting substances in 1972.

OSHA cites Dartmouth

On August 18, 1997, the Occupation Safety and Health Administration (OSHA) fined Dartmouth College $13,500 for its role in Wetterhahn's death. The agency ruled that the college had not warned its researchers about the limitations of latex (synthetic rubber or plastic) gloves. As Wetterhahn's death shows, the gloves do not adequately protect the skin from deadly compounds such as dimethyl mercury. (In tests, chemists have found that dimethyl mercury permeates disposable gloves in fifteen seconds or less.) OSHA also cited Dartmouth for not supplying other types of protection besides latex gloves. When handling dangerous compounds, OSHA suggests that scientists wear highly resistant laminate gloves (consisting of several bonded layers) under a pair of heavy-duty neoprene

Karen Wetterhahn cofounded the Women in Science Project in order to increase the number of women participating in science studies.

gloves. (Neoprene is a synthetic rubber that is highly resistant to oils and other substances. It is also used to make wet suits.)

Safety standards set

Dartmouth responded to the Wetterhahn tragedy by instituting three important changes. First, the college placed brightly colored warning stickers on boxes of latex gloves, alerting users that the gloves are not intended for use with hazardous chemicals. Next, Dartmouth officials warned other colleges and labs about the dangers of dimethyl mercury and other dangerous materials. Finally, Dartmouth instituted workshops to educate faculty and staff about proper glove selection.

As a part of its safety guidelines, OSHA also urged the scientific community to use a less dangerous chemical than dimethyl mercury in NMR spectroscopy. Researchers who practice NMR spectroscopy use dimethyl mercury because it produces a clear NMR signal. Scientists can also use inorganic mercury salt, however, which is much safer. Since the salt is a solid rather than a liquid, users face a smaller chance of inhaling or absorbing the deadly mercury.

Learning from mistakes

It is a tragic irony that a scientist who was helping to improve the environment died as a result of her efforts. Wetterhahn could be criticized for overconfidence because she was not more careful when handling a highly poisonous compound. Other scientists have concluded, however, that she probably assumed her latex gloves offered adequate protection. Researchers say that if any good can be derived from Wetterhahn's death, it is a heightened awareness in the scientific community of potential laboratory dangers. (For instance, Dartmouth College and many other research centers have instituted measures to make their laboratories safer as a result of her accident.) The rest of the world has also been reminded of the dangers associated with the use of toxic chemicals in high technology research.

FOR FURTHER REFERENCE

Periodicals

"An Avoidable Tragedy." *Occupational Hazards.* August, 1997.

"Colleagues Vow to Learn from Chemist's Death." *The New York Times.* October 3, 1997.

Picture Credits

The photographs and illustrations appearing in *Great Misadventures: Bad Ideas That Led to Big Disasters* were received from the following sources:

On the cover: *Titanic* sinking (**Painting by Willie Stoewer/UPI/Corbis-Bettmann. Reproduced by permission.**).

In the text: **Corbis-Bettmann. Reproduced by permission**: 4, 19, 35, 202, 218, 241, 284, 378, 389, 410, 447, 455, 468, 544, 586, 603; **Gustave Dore/Corbis-Bettmann. Reproduced by permission**: 10; **Archive Photos. Reproduced by permission**: 16, 27, 66, 97, 150, 153, 411, 412, 418, 436, 622, 652, 725; **Library of Congress. Reproduced by permission**: 42, 48, 105, 109, 231, 372, 406, 448, 464, 494, 565, 570, 578, 581, 588, 592, 628, 651; **The Granger Collection, New York. Reproduced by permission**: 56, 76, 115, 120, 123, 158; **Charles Nahl/Corbis-Bettmann. Reproduced by permission**: 91; **AP/Wide World Photos. Reproduced by permission**: 137, 142, 166, 176, 181, 186, 193, 210, 215, 245, 249, 257, 266, 267, 275, 290, 303, 305, 335, 339, 359, 361, 363, 367, 369, 452, 503, 505, 506, 514, 518, 530, 557, 602, 605, 630, 634, 642, 644, 646, 653, 662, 673, 682, 687, 697, 700, 706, 720, 722; **Norwegian Information Services. Reproduced by permission**: 154; **Lacy Atkins. AP/Wide World Photos. Reproduced by permission**: 176; **Archive Photos/Popperfoto. Reproduced by permission**: 200; **UPI/Corbis-Bettmann. Reproduced by permission**: 205, 226, 326, 544, 547, 616, 654; **Archive Photos/Lambert. Reproduced by permission**: 211; **Lisa Bunin/Greenpeace. Reproduced by permission**: 238; **Robert Visser/Greenpeace. Reproduced by permission**: 296; **Richard Diaz. AP/Wide World Photos. Reproduced by permission**: 303; **Peter Maksymec/AP/Wide World Photos.**

Reproduced by permission: 305; Merjenburgh/Greenpeace. Reproduced by permission: 341; Peter A. Simon/Phototake. Reproduced by permission: 352; Musee de Versailles. Reproduced by permission: 426; *Harper's Weekly*/Corbis-Bettmann. Reproduced by permission: 441; National Archives and Records Administration. Reproduced by permission: 457, 459, 596, 598; Bildarchiv Preussischer Kulturbesitz. Reproduced by permission: 477; FotoMarburg/ Art Resource. Reproduced by permission: 483; Michael St. Maur Sheil/Corbis-Bettmann. Reproduced by permission: 488; National Portrait Gallery. Reproduced by permission: 522; John F. Kennedy Library. Reproduced by permission: 531; Painting by J. L. Gerome/New York Public Library Picture Collection. Reproduced by permission: 562; National Baseball Library & Archive, Cooperstown, NY. Reproduced by permission: 608; Los Angeles Times Photographic Archive, Department of Special Collections, University Research Library, UCLA. Reproduced by permission: 639; The Kobal Collection. Reproduced by permission: 665; Doug Mills/AP/Wide World Photos. Reproduced by permission: 700; Junji Kurokawa/Corbis-Bettmann. Reproduced by permission: 714; Enny Nuraheni. Reuters/Archive Photos. Reproduced by permission: 725.

Index

Italic type indicates volume numbers; boldface type indicates entries and their page numbers; (ill.) indicates illustrations.

A

Aaron Arrowsmith and Sons *1:* 89

Abelard, Peter *4:* **567–74**, 570 (ill.)

Abolition *3:* 445–46, 449

Aborigines *1:*68, *1:* 118

Abrams, Creighton *3:* 542

Academy Award *4:* 661, 662, 666, 667

Adams, Martin *1:*183, 184

Adventure Consultants *1:* 182

Agency for Toxic Substances and Disease Registry *2:* 243

Agent Orange spraying *2:* **273–81**, 274 (ill.); *3:* 539

Agis II *3:* 373

Agnew, Spiro T. *4:* 656

Agrippa *4:* 565

Ahwelahtea *1:*139, 142

AIDS (acquired immunodeficiency syndrome) *2:* 255

Alarcón, Hernando de *1:* 35

Alberic *4:* 569

Alcibiades *3:* 371–76, 372 (ill.)

Alexander the Great *3:* **377–85**, 378 (ill.)

Algonquins *1:*49, *1:* 52

Ali *3:* 554

All the President's Men 4: 658

Allen, Woody *4:* 629

Allies *3:* 427, 429–31, 469, 475, 511–15

Almagro, Diego de *1:* 30, 31

Alvarado Construction Incorporated *4:* 672

Alvarado, Hernando de *1:* 37

Alvarado, Linda *4:* 672

Alvarado, Pedro de *1:* **24–32**, 27 (ill.)

Alvarado, Robert *4:* 672

Alyeska *2:* 343

Amalric of Lusignan *3:* 391

Amerasia 4: 627

American Civil War *3:* 445, 446, 454–55, 456

American Justice 4: 686

American League *4:* 608

American Legion *2:* 281

American Revolution *3:* 415, 455

Ames, Aldrich *4:* **675–83**, 682 (ill.)

Ames, Carleton Cecil *4:* 677

Ames, Maria del Rosario *4:* 676, 681–83

Ames, Rachel Aldrich *4:* 677

Amish *4:* 590

Amnesty International *4:* 719

Amon-Ra *3:* 379

Amritsar Massacre *3:* **496–501**

Amundsen, Roald *1:* 136, 144, 147, 150, 151, 153–55, 154 (ill.)

Anaconda Copper Mining Company *2:* 191, 193–96

Andrea Gail **sinking** *4:* **691–95**

Andreotta, Glenn *3:* 541

Anne Royal 3: 395, 397, 398

Anne, Queen of England *4:* 580, 581

Anselm of Laon *4:* 567

Antarctica *1:*72, 144

Anticommunism *4:* 626, 628, 631–32

Anzacs *3:* 471

Apocalypse Now 3: 543

Apollo 13 2: **282–88**, 284 (ill.)

Aristotle *3:* 380, 384; *4:* 573

Arkin, Alan *4:* 664

Army-McCarthy hearings *4:* 626, 631

Army of the Republic of Vietnam *3:* 537–40

Army tank *3:* 510

Arnold, Jan *1:* 189

ARTC (Air Route Traffic Control) *2:* 260, 263

Artificial heart failure *2:* **214–19**

Asahara, Shoko *4:* 711, 712, 714–15

Asch Building *4:* 601

Asinof, Elliott *4:* 614

Assault on Fort Wagner *3:* **445–53**

Asvaldsson, Thorvald *1:* 5

Atago *3:* 517

Athenians *3:* 373–74

Atlantic Richfield Company *2:* 196

Attell, Abe *4:* 610–12

Aud *3:* 489–91

Aum Shinrikyo 4: 711, 715–16

Austin, Horaţio 1: 101

Australia 1: 68

Australian Light Horse Brigade 3: 474

Auto–da–fé 4: 577

Automated Guideway Transit System 4: 674

Aviation Hall of Fame 2: 252

Axis Powers 3: 511, 512

Aztecs 1: 24, 25, 27, 28

B

Babcock & Wilcox 2: 295, 298

Balian of Ibelin 3: 391

Ballard, Robert D. 2: 207

Banks, Joseph 1: 67, 75, 81

Barents, Willem 1: **53–57**, 56 (ill.)

Barille, Edward 1: 137, 142

Baring Future Singapore 4: 703, 705

Baring, Peter 4: 707

Barings Future Singapore 4: 703

Barings PLC 4: 703–10

Barrioneuvo, Francisco de 1: 29, 30

Barry, Jack 4: 624 (ill.), 643, 646 (ill.), 647

Baseball Hall of Fame 4: 612, 613

Bass, Dick 1: 181

Batista, Fulgencio 3: 529

Battle of Brownstown 3: 415

Battle of Fallen Timbers 3: 411

Battle of Gettysburg 3: 454, 456, 459–61, 459 (ill.)

Battle of Hattin 3: **386–92**

Battle of Lake Erie 3: 416

Battle of Leyte Gulf 3: 512, 517–20

Battle of Little Bighorn 3: **463–68**

Battle of Matineia 3: 375

Battle of New Orleans 3: 424

Battle of Okinawa 3: 520

Battle of Poltava 3: **400–04**

Battle of the Thames 3: 416

Battle of Tippecanoe 3: 414

Battle of Trenton 3: **405–08**

Battle of Verdun 3: **476–86**

Battle of Waterloo 3: **425–32**

Baxter HealthCare 2: 355

Bay of Pigs invasion 3: **529–535**

Bear River 1: 83

Beckwith, Charles 3: 548–50

Beidleman, Neal 1: 183–85, 187

Belalcázar, Sebastián de 1: 30

Belcher, Edward 1: 101

Belgica 1: 136

Bell, Alexander Graham 1: 132

Bennett, James Gordon 1: 130, 131, 133

Benteen, Frederick W. 3: 467

Benton, Rube 4: 609

Bergeron, Richard 2: 346

Bering Strait 1: 129, 131, 132

Bernard of Clairvaux 4: 571, 573

Bernstein, Carl 4: 652, 652

Bessels, Emil 1: 103

Bessus 3: 379

Bhopal toxic vapor leak 2: **315–19**, 316 (ill.)

Big-budget movie mania 4: **660–68**

Bioremediation 2: 340

Bishop of Lydda 3: 391

Black Committee 3: 447, 448

Black Flags 1: 127

The Black Phalanx 3: 451

Black Sox baseball scandal 4: **607–14**, 608 (ill.)

Blanck, Max 4: 600, 606

Bligh Reef 2: 338, 339, 343

Blücher, Gebhard Leberecht von 3: 428, 430–32

Bobadilla, Francisco de 1: 22

Bock, Fedor von 3: 509

Bombimg of Hiroshima 3: 520

Bombing of Nagasaki 3: 520

Bonaparte, Napoléon 3: 425–32, 426 (ill.)

The Bonfire of the Vanities 4: 660, 663

Boots and Saddles 3: 465

Bork, Robert 4: 655

Born on the Fourth of July 3: 543

Boston Molasses spill 2: **209–13**, 210 (ill.)

Boukreev, Anatoli 1: 183–85, 188, 189

Bourbon Restoration 3: 427

Bowers, Henry 1: 149

Bradley, John R. 1: 138

Brahe, William 1: 116, 120

Brashears, David 1: 181, 188

Breen, Margaret 1: 94

Breen, Patrick 1: 94

Bre-X scandal 4: **724–29**

A Brief and True Report of the New Found Land of Virginia 1: 49

Bristol Myers Squibb 2: 355

British Board of Trade 2: 204, 206

British Commissariats 3: 436

Brock, Isaac 3: 415

Brothers, Joyce 4: 643

Brown, Belmore 1: 137

Brown, John 4: 595–99, 596 (ill.)

Brudenell, James Thomas, Earl of Cardigan 3: 438

Brué , A. H. 1: 89

BSE (bovine spongiform encephalopathy) 2: 357, 361–63

Burke, Robert O'Hara 1: **114–21**, 115 (ill.)

Burns, Sleepy Bill 4: 610, 611

Burton, Richard 1: 110, 112

Bush, George 3: 553, 558, 559

Bushido 3: 516

Butte Miner's Union 2: 194

Butterfield, Alexander 4: 653

Byrd, Richard 1: 153

C

C-16 Organized Crime Squad *4:* 684–85, 687, 688

CAA (Civil Aeronautics Administration) *2:* 259

CAB (Civil Aeronautics Board) *2:* 262–263

Cabeza de Vaca, Alvar Nuñez *1:* 34

Caesar and Cleopatra 4: 564

Caesarion *4:* 563

California Gold Rush *4:* 724

Californian 2: 206

Calley, William L. *3:* 541

Callisthenes *3:* 380

Calpurnia *4:* 563

Cameron, James *4:* 667

Cameron, Verney Lovett *1:* 113

Cantrill, Hadley *4:* 625

Carney, William H. *3:* 451

Carpathia 2: 206

Carrel, Alexis *2:* 214

Carson, Rachel *2:* 230, 232–34

Carter, Jimmy *2:* 238, 240, 242, 300; *3:* 546, 554

Cartolini, Nestor Cerpa *4:* 717–19, 722, 723

Casement, Roger *3:* 488, 491, 492, 492 (ill.), 494

Cass, Lewis *3:* 420–22

Castellano, Paul *4:* 689

Castro, Fidel *3:* 529, 530 (ill.), 531, 533

Catesby, Robert *4:* 580–82

Cayacauga 3: 417–19

Ceannt, Eamonn *3:* 489

Cecil, Edward *3:* 393, 395, 398

Center for the Biology of Natural Systems *2:* 280

Central Powers *3:* 470

CERN (European Laboratory for Particle Research) *2:* 314

Challenger explosion *2:* **320–30,** 321 (ill.), 326 (ill.)

Chambers, Whittaker *4:* 628

Chapin, Dwight *4:* 656

Charles I *4:* 580

Charles of Spain *1:* 29, 31

Charles XII *3:* 400–02

Chase, Hal *4:* 609

Chaves, Steve *4:* 672

Chemical dispersants *2:* 340

Chemie Grünenthal *2:* 254–55

Chernobyl accident *2:* **331–37,** 335 (ill.)

Chevrolet Corvair *2:* **265–72,** 266 (ill.)

Chiang Kai-shek *4:* 629

Chicago White Sox *4:* 607, 610, 614

Chicksika *3:* 410

Child Pilot Safety Act *1:* 179

Children's Crusade *1:* **7–13,** 10 (ill.)

Christmas Island *1:* 73

Chrysler Valiant *2:* 267

Chuma, James *1:* 110, 113

Churchill, Winston *3:* 500

Chuvakhin, Sergei *4:* 677, 678, 681

CIA (Central Intelligence Agency) *3:* 529, 532–34, 553, 558; *4:* 675, 680–83

Cicotte, Eddie *4:* 608, 610

Cimino, Michael *4:* 661, 662

Cincinnati Reds *4:* 607–09, 613, 614

Cirelli, Michael *4:* 686

Citizen Army *3:* 489

Citizen Kane 4: 624

Clark, William *1:* 89

Clark, Barney *2:* 214, 218 (ill.)

Clarke, Thomas *3:* 489–91

Clean Sox *4:* 607, 614

Cleopatra's fall *4:* **561–66,** 562 (ill.)

The Climb: Tragic Ambitions on Everest 1: 189

Clinton, Bill *1:* 175; *2:* 312, 349; *4:* 670

Clitus *3:* 380

CNN (Cable News Network) *3:* 558

Cobb, Ty *4:* 609, 613

Coiro, Michael *4:* 687

Colbern, Lawrence *3:* 541

Cold War (definition) *4:* 678

Collins, Michael *3:* 493

Collinson, Richard *1:* 98

Colorado River *1:* 87, 88

Colson, Charles *4:* 656

Columbia River Territory *1:* 87–88

Columbia 2: 322

Columbus, Bartholomeo *1:* 19, 21

Columbus, Christopher *1:* **14–23,** 16 (ill.)

Columbus, Diego *1:* 22

Columbus, Fernando *1:* 19, 22

Comiskey, Charles *4:* 607, 610–12

Commoner, Barry *2:* 280

Communism *3:* 521–23, 527, 539, 543

Communist Party *4:* 627–29, 635, 638

Confederacy *3:* 454, 462, 463–64

Confederate States of America *3:* 446

Connally, John *4:* 656

Connolly, James *3:* 489, 491, 493

Conquistadors (definition) *1:* 24

Continental Army *3:* 406

Contras *3:* 551

Cook Strait *1:* 68

Cook, Frederick Albert *1:* **135–43,** 137 (ill.), 142 (ill.)

Cook, James *1:* **65–74,** 66 (ill.)

Cooley, Denton *2:* 215

Cooper's Creek *1:* 115, 117, 118, 120

Copper mining in Butte, Montana *2:* **191–97**

Coronado, Francisco Vázquez de
1: 33–39, 35 (ill.)

Cortés, Hernán 1: 26–28, 31

Cosa Nostra 4: 686, 687

Cosco, Doug 4: 692

Costner, Kevin 4: 665–667

Cousins, Gregory 2: 339, 342

Coutts and Company 4: 704

Cowan, Lou 4: 641

Cox, Archibald 4: 653–55

Cox, Geraldine 2: 241

Craterus 3: 381

Crazy Horse 3: 467, 468, 468 (ill.)

CREEP (Committee to Reelect the
President) 4: 651–52, 656

Creutzfeldt-Jakob disease 2: 360–61

Crimean War 3: 433–39

Croatoan 1: 51

Crowe, Gary 4: 699

Crowe, Robert 4: 612

Crusades 1: 8; 3: 386–87, 391, 392

Cuban Brigade 3: 529, 532–34

Cuban missile crisis 3: 534

Cunard Line 2: 199 199

Curtiss School of Aviation 1: 158

Custer, Elizabeth Bacon 3: 465

Custer, George Armstrong 3:
463–68, 464 (ill.)

D

Dafoe, Allan Roy 4: 615, 616

Dáil Eireann 3: 493

Daly, Marcus 2: 193

Dances with Wolves 4: 665–66

Dare, Virginia 1: 50

Darius III 3: 378, 379

Dartmouth College 2: 365, 368

Darwin, Charles 1: 70

Davis, Jefferson 3: 454, 455, 464

D.C. Year 2000 Group 2: 348

DDT (dichloro diphenyl
trichloroethane) contamination
2: **230–36**, 231 (ill.), 233 (ill.)

De Guzman, Michael 4: 725, 729

De Long, Emma Wotton 1: 130,
132, 134

**De Long, George Washington
1: 129–34**

De Palma, Brian 4: 663, 664

De Valera, Eamon 3: 494,
494 (ill.), 495

Dean, John 4: 652, 653,
654 (ill.), 656

DeBakey, Michael 2: 215

Deep Throat 4: 658

The Deer Hunter 3: 543; 4: 661

Delian League 3: 372

Demosthenes 3: 373–75

Denby, David 4: 665

**Denver International Airport
construction 4: 669–74,
673 (ill.)**

Derivatives 4: 704, 705, 707–09

Derounian, Steve 4: 648

Desert Base One 3: 548

Devereux, Robert 1: 42; 3: 396

Devries, William C. 2: 217, 219

Dias, Bartolomeu 1: 16

Díaz, Melchor 1: 35

Diem, Ngo Dinh 3: 537

Dinkins, David 4: 664

The Dionne Quints: Family Secrets
4: 619

**Dionne quintuplets 4: 615–20,
616 (ill.)**

Dioxin 2: 273, 278, 281

Discoverie of Guiana 1: 44

Discovery (ship) : 72, 73, 146

Discovery (shuttle) 2: 322

DIY (Do It Yourself) 4: 590

DNC (Democratic National
Committee) 4: 650, 651

Doar, John 4: 657

Donner Party 1: 90–95, 91 (ill.)

Dorrell, Stephen 2: 361

Doudart de Lagrée, Ernest 1: 126

Douglass, Frederick 3: 445,
448 (ill.); 4: 596

Dow Chemical Corporation 2: 278,
353–55

Drake, Francis 1: 49

Dr. Zhivago 4: 666

**Dubroff, Jessica 1: 174–79,
176 (ill.)**

Dubroff, Lloyd 1: 174–76, 178, 179

Dummar, Melvin 2: 251

Dupuis, Jean 1: 126, 127

Dutch Arctic Enterprise 1: 53, 54

Dyer, Reginald E. H. 3: 496–500

E

**Earhart, Amelia 1: 157–63,
158 (ill.)**

Easter Rising 3: 487–95

Ebierbing, Joe 1: 103

Ebierbing, Tookolito 1: 103

Eckardt, Shawn 4: 699

Eckener, Hugo 2: 220, 228

*The Edgar Bergen and Charlie
McCarthy Show* 4: 623

Edison, Thomas 1: 132

Ehrlichman, John 4: 652, 656

Eight Men Out 4: 614

Eisenhower, Dwight D. 2: 259, 263;
3: 530, 537; 4: 631, 644

El Dorado 1: 42, 44

Elitcher, Max 4: 637, 4: 638

Elizabeth I 1: 40–41, 42 (ill.), 49;
3: 395; 4: 580, 582

Ellsberg, Daniel 4: 656, 657

Ellsworth, Lincoln 1: 153

Emancipation Proclamation 3: 446

Emergency Position Indicating
Radio Beacon 4: 693

The Emigrants' Guide to Oregon and California 1: 91

The Empire Strikes Back 4: 660

Endeavour (ship) *1*: 66, 70, 71, 74

Endeavour (shuttle) *2*: 330

Endecott, John *4*: 578

Endo, Seiichi *4*: 716

English expedition to Cádiz 3*: 393–99

Enright, Dan *4*: 643, 644, 646

Enterprise 1: 98

EPA (Environmental Protection Agency) *2*: 196, 231, 234, 279–80

Erik (the Red) *1*: 1–6, 4 (ill.)

Erikkson, Leif *1*: 1, 4

Ervin, Samuel J. *4*: 653

Espionage *4*: 633, 636, 639

Essex 3: 532

Estevanico *1*: 33–34, 36

Estigarriba, General *3*: 441

Estrada, Beatriz de *1*: 38

Etukishook *1*: 139, 142

European Union *2*: 361, 363

Evans, Edgar *1*: 149

Evans, Nat *4*: 611

Everest, Mount (fatalities on) *1*: 180–90, 185 (ill.)

Ewell, Richard *3*: 457, 459

Explorers Club *1*: 138, 143

Exxon Baton Rouge *2*: 340

Exxon *Valdez* oil spill *2*: 338–44, 341 (ill.)

Eyre, Edward John *1*: 70

F

FAA (Federal Aviation Administration) *2*: 259, 263; *4*: 672

Fall of Athens *3*: 371–76

Fall of Detroit *3*: 417–24

Fallon, William A. *4*: 611

Fanny Hyde 1: 132

Fatal Impact 1: 70

Fatouma, Ahmadi *1*: 81

Fawkes, Guy *4*: 580–81

FBI (Federal Bureau of Investigation) *4*: 628, 636, 637, 651, 671, 672, 676, 681, 686, 699

FCC (Federal Communications Commission) *2*: 198, 208

FDA (Food and Drug Administration) *2*: 255–57, 351, 352, 355

Felderhof, John *4*: 725, 727, 729

Felsch, Oscar "Happy" *4*: 608, 609

Ferdinand, Archduke Francis *3*: 470

Ferdinand, King *1*: 16, 21

Fermi National Accelerator Laboratory *2*: 314

Ferrer, Fernando *4*: 664

Fidelity Investments *4*: 727

54th Massachusetts Regiment *3*: 445–51

Field of Dreams 4: 666

Fiennes, Ralph *4*: 648

Filder, General *3*: 436

Fire code regulations *2*: 302, 305, 307, 308

Fischbeck, Frank *1*: 183, 184

Fischer, Scott *1*: 180–90, 181 (ill.)

Fish-Eaters *3*: 382

Fitzgerald, F. Scott *4*: 611

Ford, Gerald R. *4*: 658, 659

Ford Falcon *2*: 267

Ford Pinto *2*: 289–94, 290 (ill.)

Fox, Charlotte *1*: 183

Franck, Rudolph *1*: 139

Franco-Prussian War *1*: 122

Frankfurter, Felix *4*: 647

Franklin, Jane *1*:98, 101

Franklin, John *1*: 96–103, 97 (ill.)

Frederick Douglass's Paper 3: 447

Freedman, Al *4*: 644, 645, 647

Freedman's Colony *1*: 51

Freeman, Morgan *4*: 664

Freeman, Orville *2*: 234

Freeport McMoRan Copper and Gold *4*: 726–28

French Indochina War *3*: 536

French Revolution *4*: 587

Friendship 1: 159

The Front 4: 629

Frye, Ralph *2*: 212

Fuchs, Klaus *4*: 629, 634, 636, 637, 639

Fujimori, Alberto *4*: 717, 720, 723

Fukudome, Shigeru *3*: 516, 518

Fulbright, James William *3*: 540

G

Gabriel, George *4*: 685, 688

Gajdusek, D. Carleton *2*: 360, 363

Gallien, Jim *1*: 168, 170

Gallipoli (film) *3*: 474

Gallipoli campaign *3*: 469–75

Gallipoli Peninsula *3*: 469, 471

Gambia River *1*: 76, 80

Gambino, Tommy *4*: 685

Gamma-Electron-Muon detector *2*: 313

Gammelgaard, Lene *1*: 183, 187

Gandhi, Mohandas *3*: 499, 500, 500 (ill.)

Gandhi, Rajiv *2*: 319

Gandil, Charles "Chick" *4*: 608

Ganz, Joachim *1*: 49

Gardner, John *1*: 85

Garnier, Francis *1*: 122–28, 123 (ill.)

Gau, Makalu *1*: 188

General Accounting Office 4: 671

General Motors 2: 265, 268, 271

Geneva Accords 3: 537

George, Clair 4: 679

Gerard of Ridefort 3: 388

Geritol 4: 643

Germ warfare 4: 711, 715, 716

Gettysburg Address 3: 461

Gettysburg National Military Park
   3: 461

Gibbs, Lois 2: 239, 241 (ill.)

Gibson, Mel 3: 474

Gilbert, Humphrey 1: 40–41

Gillmore, George 3: 452

Gillooly, Jeff 4: 696–97, 701

Giusi, Carlos 4: 723

Glaspie, April 3: 556, 558

Glory 2: 452 (ill.), 453

Goeldi, Anne 4: 579

Gold, Harry 4: 635–38

Gomery, Adrien Gerlache de 1: 136

Gone with the Wind 4: 666

Good, Dorcas 4: 579

Good, Sarah 4: 579

Goodwin, Richard 4: 647, 649

Gorbachev, Mikhail 2: 332; 4: 681

Gotti, John 4: **684–90**, 687 (ill.)

Government Committee on
   Operations 4: 631, 632

Graf Zeppelin 2: 221, 222, 224, 228

Grant, Ulysses S. 3: 455

Gravano, Salvatore 4: 686

Gray, Charles 1: 116, 118

The Great Gatsby 4: 611

Great Salt Lake 1: 85, 85, 87

Great Southern Continent
   1: 66, 68

Greater East Asia Co-Prosperity
   Sphere 3: 513

Greenglass, David 4: 635, 635–38

Greenglass, Ruth 4: 635, 638

Greenland 1: 1, 3

Gregory IX 1: 11

Grenville, Richard 1: 42

Griffith, Melanie 4: 663

Griffon 1: 58, 60

Grijalva, Juan de 1: 31

Grimes, Sandy 4: 679, 681

Groom, Mike 1: 183, 185, 188

Grouchy, Emmanuel de 3: 428,
   430, 431

Guinness Book of Records 1: 175

Gulf of Carpentaria 1: 116

Gulf of Tonkin Resolution 3: 538

Gummer, John 2: 361

Gunpowder Plot 4: **580–84**,
   583 (ill.)

Guy of Lusignan 3: 386, 388, 391

Gylippus 3: 373, 375

H

Haise, Fred W. 2: 283, 285, 287

Hakim 3: 387

Haldeman, H. R. 4: 652, 656, 657

Hall, Charles Francis 1:103, 129

Hall, Rob 1: 180–90

Halsey, William F. 3: 519, 520

Hamilton, Ian 3: 469, 470, 473, 474

"The Hammer of Witches" (see
   Malleus Maleficarum)

Hammer, Armand 2: 241

Hammond Iron Works 2: 209, 211

Hanks, Tom 4: 663

Hansen, Doug 1: 183

Harana, Diego de 1: 18

Harding, Al 4: 698

Harding, Lavona 4: 698

Harding, Tonya 4: **696–702**,
   697 (ill.), 700 (ill.)

Harland & Wolff 2: 199

Harpers Ferry 4: 595–99, 598 (ill.)

Harriot, Thomas 1: 49

Harris, Andy 1: 183-84

Harris, Isaac 4: 600, 606

Harrison, William Henry 3: 412

Hart, Frederick 3: 544

Hastings, Lansford 1: 91

Hathaway, Lisa Blair 1:174, 175

Hawaiian Islands 1:65, 73

Hazelwood, Joseph 2: 338,
   339 (ill.), 342, 344

Hearst, William Randolph 4: 624

Heaven's Gate 4: 660–62, 662 (ill.),
   666, 667

Heemskerck, Jacob van 1: 53, 56

Helga 3: 492

Hell's Angels 2: 246, 251

Héloïse 4: **567–74**, 570 (ill.)

Henry III of England 3: 391

Herbert, Wally 1: 141

Herclides 3: 383

Hess, Rudolf 3: 504

Hessians 3: 405

Hibbins, Anne 4: 578

Hibbins, William 4: 578

Hillary Step 1: 181, 182, 185

Hillary, Edmund 1: 181

Hindenburg, Paul von 2: 222

***Hindenburg* crash** 2: **220–29**,
   221 (ill.), 226 (ill.)

Hispaniola 1: 14, 17, 19, 22, 23

Hiss, Alger 4: 628, 628 (ill.)

Historia calamitatum 4: 568, 572

History of the World 1: 41, 44

Hitler, Adolf 3: 502, 503 (ill.), 505,
   507–09; 4: 634

HIV (human immunodeficiency
   virus) 2: 255

Ho Chi Minh 3: 537

Hoffman, Dustin 4: 658

Holloway Special Operations Review
   Group 3: 551

Hollywood Ten 4: 629

Holy City *1:* 8

Holy Land *1:* 8–9, 11, 12; *3:* 386, 387, 392

Hooker Chemical Corporation *2:* 237, 240, 241

Hopper, Dennis *4:* 665

Hospital for Sick Children *4:* 615

Hostage crisis in Peru *4:* **717–23,** 720 (ill.), 722 (ill.)

Houghton, Daniel *1:* 76–77

House Un-American Activities Committee *4:* 628, 629

Howard Hughes Medical Institute *2:* 251

Howard, Edward Lee *4:* 679

Howe, William *3:* 406

Howitt, Alfred *1:* 119, 120

Hudson's Bay Company *1:* 83, 88–89

Hugh IX *3:* 391

Hugh VIII *3:* 391

Hugh X *3:* 391

Hughes Aircraft Company *2:* 246, 251

Hughes Tool Company *2:* 244

Hughes, Howard *2:* **244–52,** 245 (ill.)

Hull, William *3:* 415, 417, 418 (ill.)

Humboldt River *1:* 87

Hundred Days *3:* 427, 432

Hunter Commission *3:* 496, 500

Hurricane Grace *4:* 691

Hussein, Saddam *3:* 553, 560

Hutchinson, Stuart *1:* 183, 184

I

Idaho National Engineering Laboratory *2:* 301

ILGW (International Ladies Garment Workers) *4:* 606

Incans *1:*24, 28

Indian Supreme Court *2:* 317

Industrial Revolution *4:* 585–87

Infantry charge *3:* 430

Innocent III *1:* 9

Institute of Nuclear Power Operations (INPO) *2:* 301

Inter-American Commission on Human Rights *4:* 719

International Ice Patrol *2:* 198, 207

Into Thin Air 1: 189, 190

Intrepid 1: 101

Invasion from Mars 4: 625

Investigator 1: 98–100

Iran-Contra affair *3:* 551

Iran hostages *3:* 546– 547, 547 (ill.)

Iran-Iraq war *3:* 555

Irish Republican Army *3:* 493

Irish Republican Brotherhood *3:* 489

Irish Volunteers *3:* 489, *3:* 490

Iron Hugo *1:* 11

Iroquois *1:* 59

Irving, Clifford *2:* 251

Isaaco *1:* 79

Isabella, Queen *1:* 16, 21, 22

Ishii, Tomoko *4:* 712

Ismay, J. Bruce *2:* 199, 202

The *Italia* crash *1:* **151–56**

Itsaca 1: 162

Iwo Jima *2:* 287

IWW (International Workers of the World) 2: 191, 194

J

Morgan, J. P. *4:* 727

Jackson, Andrew *3:* 424

Jackson, Joe ("Shoeless Joe") *4:* 608–10, 614

Jackson, Thomas "Stonewall" *3:* 456, 457

Jager, Peter de *2:* 346

James I *1:* 44; *4:* 580–81, 581 (ill.)

Jarvik, Robert *2:* 215 (ill.), 216, 217

Jarvik-7 *2:* 214, 218, 219

Jarvik-3 *2:* 217

Jarvis, Gregory *2:* 324

Jaworski, Leon *4:* 655–57

Jeannette 1: 129, 131–34

Jefferson, Thomas *3:* 418

Jenkinson, Robert Banks *4:* 589

Jersey Central Power and Light Company *2:* 296

Jesus of Nazareth *1:* 7, 8

Jett, Joseph *4:* 709

John Brown's raid *3:* **595–99**

Johnson, Lyndon B. *2:* 270; *3:* 538, 542; *4:* 659

Jolliet, Louis *1:* 59, 62

Joséphine *3:* 427

Julius Caesar *4:* 561

Junger, Sebastian *4:* 694

K

Kaczynski, David *4:* 590

Kaczynski, Theodore *4:* 590

Kaiser, Henry John *2:* 247

Kaiser, John *2:* 247

Kamikaze at Leyte Gulf *3:* **512–20,** 514 (ill.), 518 (ill.)

Kasischke, Lou *1:* 183

Kaufman, Irving *4:* 639

Kefauver-Harris Act *2:* 257

Kelsey, Frances Oldham *2:* 256, 258

Kemeny Report *2:* 300

Kemys, Lawrence *1:* 45

Kennedy, John F. *2:* 234, 257, 275; *3:* 530, 531 (ill.), 534, 535, 537, 538; *4:* 600

Kennedy, Robert F. *3:* 540

Kerrigan, Nancy *4:* 696, 700 (ill.), 701, 702

Keseberg, Lewis *1:* 95

KGB *4:* 675

Khomeini, Ayatollah Ruhollah
   3: 546–47, 554

Khrushchev, Nikita 3: 534

Kidder Peabody 4: 709

King Baldwin IV 3: 391

King Edward VII Land 1: 144, 145

King, John 1: 116, 119, 120

Kinkaid, Thomas 3: 517

Kissinger, Henry 3: 542

Kitchener, Herbert Horatio 3: 472

Kittson, William 1: 85

Kleindienst, Richard 4: 652

Kleist, Paul von 3: 509

Koch, Howard 4: 621

Kolff, Willem 2: 215, 218

Korean War 3: 521, 522, 523,
   524–28

Kostner, Kevin 4: 665, 665 (ill.),
   666, 667

Kovic, Ron 3: 543

Krakauer, Jon 1: 180, 184, 188, 189

Krämer, Henry 4: 575

Kravec, John 4: 685, 686

Kremer, Semion 4: 634

Kristofferson, Kris 4: 661

Kruse, Dale 1: 183

Kurita, Vice Admiral 3: 516–19

Kuru 2: 360, 363

Kwann-Gett, Clifford S. 2: 217

Kyle, James H. 3: 549, 550

L

Lagrée, Ernest Doudart de 1: 124

Lalawethika 3: 410, 412, 412 (ill.)

Lancet 2: 360

Landis, Kenesaw Mountain 4: 613

Lane, Ralph 1: 49

Langlois, Bertrand Dionne 4: 619

Lanier, Jaron 2: 347

La Salle, René-Robert de 1: 58–64

Las Casas, Bartolomé de 1: 20

Latin Kingdom of Jerusalem 3: 387

Lattimore, Owen 4: 631

Lavoisier, Antoine-Laurent 2: 368

Lawrence, Ernest Orlando 2: 310

Ledyard, John 1: 76

Lee, Debra 4: 694

Lee, Robert E. 3: 454, 457 (ill.),
   458, 461; 4: 598

Leeson, Lisa 4: 707, 708

Leeson, Nicholas 4: 703–10,
   706 (ill.)

Lewenhaupt, General 3: 400–03

Lewis, Edmonia 3: 453

Lewis, Merriweather 1: 89

Liddy, G. Gordon 4: 656

Liman von Sanders, Otto 3: 470

Lin, Maya 3: 544

Lincoln, Abraham 3: 446, 447 (ill.),
   461; 4: 596

Lindbergh, Charles 2: 214

Linschoten, van Jan 1: 55

Liotta, Domingo 2: 215

Little, Frank 2: 194

Livingstone, David 1: 104–13,
   105 (ill.)

Livingstone, Mary Moffat 1: 105,
   106, 108, 110

Locascio, Frank 4: 687-89

Lockheed Constellation 2: 244,
   246–47, 250, 251

Longstreet, James 3: 456

López, Carlos Antonio 3: 442

López, Francisco Solano 3:
   440–44, 441 (ill.)

Lotulf of Rheims 4: 571

Louis XIV of France 1: 62

Louisiana Purchase 4: 703

Love Canal 2: 237–43, 238 (ill.)

Love Canal Homeowners'
   Association 2: 239, 241

Lovell, James A. 2: 283, 287

Lucas, George 4: 660

Lucas, Simon 1: 76

Ludd, Ned 4: 585, 587, 590

The Luddite movement 4: 585–90,
   586 (ill.), 588 (ill.)

Luftwaffe 3: 505, 511

Lyford, Don 2: 268

Lyman, Howard 2: 362

Lymarchus 3: 372, 373

Lynch, Eliza 3: 440, 442, 444

Lysander 3: 372

LZ 130 2: 224

M

MacArthur, Douglas 3: 521–28,
   522 (ill.)

MacDermott, Sean 3: 489, 491

Macdonnell, James 3: 429, 430

MacGillivray, Greg 1: 188

MacNeill, Eoin 3: 489, 491, 494

Mad cow disease outbreak 2:
   357–64, 358 (ill.), 361 (ill.),
   363 (ill.)

Madison, James 3: 422

Madsen, Tim 1: 183

Mafia 4: 684, 689

Maharg, Bill 4: 610

Mahlum, Charlotte 2: 354

Major, John 4: 708

Majorino, Tina 4: 665

Maldonado, Alonzo del Castillo
   1: 36

Malleus Maleficarum 4: 575–77

Managing 00: Surviving the Year 2000
   Computing Crisis 2: 346

Manhattan Project 4: 635, 637

Mao Tsetung 3: 525, 527

Maoris 1: 68

Marc Antony 4: 561, 564–66,
   565 (ill.)

Marie Louise 3: 427

Markham, Beryl 1: 160

Markievicz, Constance 3: 494

Marmar, Josiah 3: 411

Marquette, Jacques 1: 59, 62

Martinez, Colonel 3: 443

Marty 4: 645

Marx, Karl 4: 637

Mary, Queen of Scots 4: 581, 582

Massachussetts Supreme Court
2: 209, 212, 213

Mattingly, Thomas K. 2: 283

Maxwell, John 3: 493, 494

Mayas 1:24, 28

McArthur, Colonel 3: 420–23

McAuliffe, Christa 2: 321, 323–25

McBride, William 2: 255, 256

McCandless, Christopher
1: **164–72**, 166 (ill.)

The McCarthy Communist scare
4: **626–32**

McCarthy, Eugene J. 3: 540

McCarthy, Joseph R. 4: 626, 627,
629–32, 630 (ill.)

McClintock, Francis Leopold
1: 101, 102

McClure, Robert 1:96, 99, 100

McCord, James 4: 650, 656

McCutcheon, Richard 4: 642, 643

McDonald's 2: 362

McFarlane, Robert 3: 551

McGovern, George S. 3: 540; 4: 651

McGraw, John 4: 609

McKay, Thomas 1: 85

McKinley, Mount 1: 135, 137

McMullin, Fred 4: 609, 611, 613

McNair, Ronald 2: 324

McNeill, John 3: 435, 436

Meade, George 3: 460, 461

Meet the Press 2: 241

Meiji restoration 3: 516

Mein Kampf 3: 504

Melville, George 1: 133

Melvin and Howard 2: 251

The Memoirs of Howard Hughes
2: 251

"Men of Color, To Arms!" 3: 447

Mendoza, Antonio de 1: 33, 36, 38

Mercury poisoning 2: 365, 367

Mercury Theatre 4: 621

Methoataske 3: 410

Methyl isocyanate 2: 315

Metropolitan Edison 2: 296

MGM Grand Hotel fire 2: **302–08**,
303 (ill.), 305 (ill.)

Michael Collins 3: 493

Michelson, Carl 2: 298

Million Dollar Babies 4: 620

Mislock, Raymond Jr. 4: 680

Missouri Compromise 3: 455

Mitchell, John 4: 652–53,
653 (ill.), 656

Mitchell, William 3: 523

Mixtecs 1: 28

Moffett, James R. 4: 726

Mojave 1: 87

Monteagle, Lord 4: 582

Montezuma II 1: 26–27

Moorman, James 2: 242

Morehead, Alan 1: 70

Moreton Bay 1: 68

Morgan Stanley 4: 704

Morrison, Herb 2: 229

Morton Thiokol 2: 324, 329

Motor Trend 2: 268

Mountain Madness 1: 182, 188

Muhammad, Reza Shah Pahlevi
3: 547, 554

Müller, Paul 2: 231

Munro, Charles 3: 475

Muow, Bruce 4: 684–85

Murphy, Dale "Murph" 4: 694, 695

Murray, Mungo 1: 105

Mushashi 3: 518

Mussolini, Benito 1:154, 156

My Attainment of the Pole 1: 142

My Lai massacre 3: 541, 542

My Life on the Plains 3: 465

N

Nader, Ralph 2: 265, 267 (ill.), 270

Namba, Yasuko 1:183, 185, 187

Nansen, Fridtjof 1: 134

Napoléon I (see Bonaparte,
Napoléon)

Napoléon II 3: 427

Napoléon III 1: 126

Narvaez, Pánfilo 1: 26, 27

NASA (National Aeronautics and
Space Administration) 2: 282,
283, 287, 320, 322-24, 327

National Antarctic Expedition
1: 147

National Baseball Commission
4: 612

National Front for the Liberation of
Vietnam 3: 537, 539, 540,
542, 543

National Geographic Society 1: 141

National Highway Traffic Safety
Administration 2: 269

National League 4: 608

National Security Council 3: 551

National Traffic and Motor Vehicle
Safety Act 2: 265, 270

National Traffic Safety Agency
2: 269

Nazi party 3: 504

Nearchus 3: 381, 383

Nelson, Horatio 3: 440

Neo-Luddites 4: 585, 589

Nerve gas 4: 711, 713, 715, 716

Neversweat Mine 2: 193

New York draft riots 3: 446–46

New York Giants 4: 609

New York Herald 1: 129–131, 133

New York University Law School
4: 601

Ney, Michel 3: 428, 431

Niagara Falls Board of Education 2: 240

Nicholas I 3: 433

Nicias 3: 371

Niesciur, Daniel 4: 679

Niger River 1: 75, 77, 78, 81

Nightingale, Florence 3: 436 (ill.), 437

Nightmover 4: 681, 682

Nikkei index 4: 706, 707

Nimitz 3: 548

Niña 1: 17

Nixon, Richard M. 2: 234; 3: 542; 4: 628, 651, 651 (ill.), 653–55, 657–59

Niza, Fray Marcos de 1: 33-35

Nobile, Umberto 1: 151–56, 153 (ill.)

Noche Triste 1: 27

Noonan, Fred J. 1:157, 162

Norbert of Premontre 4: 571

Nor'easter 4: 691

Norge 1: 153, 154

Norplant contraceptive 2: 352

North Island 1: 68

North, Oliver 3: 551

North Pole 1: 129, 134, 135, 151, 154

North West Company 1: 84, 88

Northwest Passage 1: 72, 74, 96, 97, 99, 102

Northwest Territory 3: 411

NRC (Nuclear Regulatory Commission) 2: 298–300

Nuclear power 2: 295, 297, 301, 331, 334

O

O'Brien, Lawrence 4: 651

Occidental Petroleum Corporation 2: 241

OCD (obsessive compulsive disorder) 2: 244, 250

Octavia 4: 565

Octavian 4: 563, 565–66

Ogden, Peter Skene 1: 83–89

Ohio County Women's Republican Club 4: 626

Ohio militia 3: 423

Oil Pollution Act of 1990 2: 343

Ojeda, Alonso de 1: 18, 19

Olin Chemical Company 2: 235

Olympias 3: 384

Olympic 2: 199, 201

One-Ton Depot 1: 148, 148, 150

Onizuka, Ellison 2: 324

OPEC (Organization of Petroleum Exporting Countries) 3: 555

Operation Barbarossa 3: 502–11, 505 (ill.), 506 (ill.)

Operation Desert Shield 3: 556

Operation Desert Storm 3: 556, 558

Operation Eagle Claw 3: 546–52

Orange County, California 4: 709

Oregon Territory 1: 88

Oregon Trail 1: 87, 88, 91

O-rings 2: 320

Osborne, Sarah 4: 579

OSHA (Occupation Safety and Health Administration) 2: 368

Oswell, William Colton 1: 105–08

The Outlaw 2: 251

Ovando, Nicolas de 1: 23

Ozawa, Jisaburo 3: 519, 520

P

Pachetha 3: 410

Padilla, Fray Juan de 1: 36

Paigen, Beverly 2: 242

Paine, Thomas 4: 588

Pappenheimer, Anna 4: 577

Pappenheimer, Paul 4: 577

Paracelsus 2: 368

Paraclete 4: 568, 572–74

Paraguayan War 3: 440, 442, 444

Park, Mungo 1: 75–82, 76 (ill.)

Park, Thomas 1: 82

Parmenion 3: 378

Payne, Dan 4: 680, 4: 681

Pearl Harbor 3: 509, 513

Pearse, Patrick 3: 488 (ill.), 489–91

Peary, Robert Edward 1: 135, 136, 140–41, 143

The People 1: 39

Peloponnesian League 3: 372

Peloponnesian War 3: 371, 372, 376

Pena, Federico 4: 669, 670

Pennsylvania Electric Company 2: 296

Pepper, Benjamin 4: 679

Percy, Thomas 4: 581, 582

The Perfect Storm 4: 694–95

Pericles 3: 375

Perl, William 4: 638

Persian Gulf War 3: 553–60

Persian Wars 3: 372

Peter I (the Great) 3: 402

Peter the Venerable 4: 574

Petermann, August 1: 129, 130, 132

Petroleum Industry Response Organization 2: 343

Pharnbazus 3: 376

Philadelphia Centennial Exhibition 2: 192

Philadelphia Phillies 4: 613

Philip Augustus 1: 7, 8

Philip II 3: 384

Pickett, George Edward 3: 455 (ill.), 456, 460–61

Pickett's Charge 3: 454–62

Pied Piper of Hamlin 1: 12

Pierini, Rose 2: 269

Pindar 3: 384

Pinta 1: 17

Pirie, Lord 2: 199

Pittman, Sandy Hill 1: 180, 187

Pizarro, Francisco 1: 29, 30

Plunkett, Joseph 3: 489, 493

Plutarch 4: 563, 564

Poindexter, John 3: 551

Polaris 1: 103, 129

The Postman 4: 667

Potawototi 1: 59

Prince William Sound 2: 338, 340, 343, 344

Proctor and Gamble Company 4: 709

Project Ranch Hand 2: 275, 278

Pruss, Max 2: 224, 227, 228

Ptolemy XI 4: 561, 564

Ptolemy XIII 4: 563, 564

Ptolemy XII 4: 561, 563

Puckeshinwa 3: 409

Purity Distilling Company 2: 209, 213

Putnam, George Palmer 1: 159, 160

Q

Quintland 4: 615, 619

Quiz Show 4: 648

R

Rae, John 1: 101

Raleigh, Sir Walter 1: 40–46, 41 (ill.)

Rall, Johann Gottlieb 3: 405–06, 408

Ramotobi 1: 105

Randall, Adam 4: 692

Rao, P. V. Narasimha 2: 319

Rawlinson, Diane 4: 697, 699

Ray, Thomas (Pete) 3: 533

Raymond of Tripoli 3: 388, 391

RBMK nuclear reactor 2: 332–34, 337

Readick, Frank 4: 623

Reagan, Ronald 2: 320, 327; 3: 551-51, 553

Redford, Robert 4: 658

Redmon, Paul 4: 680

Redstone Arsenal 2: 235

Reed, James 1: 90, 94

Reed, Margaret 1: 94

Reed, Virginia 1: 93

Rehnskold, Karl Gustaf 3: 400–02, 404

Reid, Joe 1: 174,en>78

Reno, Jonet 4: 682

Reno, Marcus 3: 467

Resnick, Judith 2: 324

Resolution 1: 71,en>74

Resource Conservation and Recovery Act 2: 242

Return of the Jedi 4: 660

Reunion 4: 617

Revlon 4: 642, 643

Reynolds, Kevin 4: 665, 666

Rhee, Syngman 3: 524

Rhodes, Richard 2: 363–64

Ribicoff, Abraham 2: 269, 270

Richardson, Elliot 4: 655

Richardson-Merrel 2: 256

Risberg, Charles "Swede" 4: 608, 609

Roanoke Colony 1: 47–52, 48 (ill.)

Robards, Jason 2: 251

Robin Hood, Prince of Thieves 4: 665, 666

Rodino, Peter 4: 657

Rogers, William B. 2: 328

Rogers Commission 2: 320, 328–29

Rogovin Report 2: 300

Roosevelt, Eleanor 1: 160

Roosevelt, Franklin D. 1: 52, 135, 143; 2: 251

Rose, Pete 4: 613

The Rosenberg case 3: 633–40, 639

Rosenberg, Ethel 4: 633, 634–40, 634 (ill.)

Rosenberg, Julius 4: 633, 634–40, 634 (ill.)

Rosenhouse, Martin 4: 643

Ross, James Clark 1: 98, 101

Ross, John 1: 100–02

Roswell Cancer Institute 2: 242

Rothstein, Arnold 4: 610–12

Routhier, Daniel 4: 617

Roxana 3: 380, 384

Royal Society 1: 65, 68, 147

Ruckelhaus, William 4: 655

Rundstedt, Karl von 3: 509

Rusk, Dean 2: 275

Russell, W. H. 3: 435

S

Safety of Life at Sea conference 2: 206

Saint–Gaudens, Augustus 3: 453

Saladin 3: 386, 389 (ill.), 390, 391

Salt Lake 1:83

Samurai 3: 512, 513

Sandwich Islands 1: 73

Santa Maria 1: 17, 18

"Saturday Night Massacre" 4: 655

Satyagraha 3: 499

Saunders, Eugene 4: 699

Sauwaseekau 3: 410, 411

Saxbe, William 4: 655

Sayles, John 4: 614

Saypol, Irving 4: 638

Scarface 2: 251

Schindler's List 4: 666

Schoening, Klev 1: 183, 187

Schroeder, William 2: 219

Schwarzkopf, Norman 3: 556, 557, 557 (ill.)

Scobee, Francis 2: 323

Scott, Kathleen Bruce 1: 147

Scott, Robert Falcon 1: **144–50,** 150 (ill.)

Scrapie 2: 359, 360

Sebituane 1: 107

Second Treaty of Fort Laramie 3: 464, 465

Securities and Exchange Commission 4: 671

Seiffert, Edward R. 3: 548

Sekelutu 1: 108

Senate Banking Committee 4: 671

Senate Committee on Foreign Relations 4: 630, 632

Serious Fraud Office 4: 708

Seven Cities of Cibola 1: 33–35

Shasta, Mount 1: 86

Shaw Memorial 3: 453

Shaw, Anna Kneeland (Haggerty) 3: 449

Shaw, Francis G. 3: 448, 449, 451

Shaw, George Bernard 4: 564

Shaw, Robert Gould 3: 445, 448, 451

Shaw, Sarah Blake (Sturgis) 3: 449

Sherpa, Arita 1: 183

Sherpa, Big Pemba 1: 183

Sherpa, Chuldum 1: 183

Sherpa, Kami 1: 183

Sherpa, Lopsang Jangbu 1: 183, 187, 189

Sherpa, Ngawang Norbu 1: 183

Sherpa, Ngawang Sya Kya 1: 183

Sherpa, Ngawang Tendi 1: 183

Sherpa, Ngawang Topche 1: 183

Sherpa, Tashi Tshering 1: 183, 187

Sherpa, Tenzing 1: 183

Sherwood Foresters 3: 492

Shiite Muslims 3: 554, 555, 557

Sho l 3: 516–17

Sic et non 4: 571

Sidorovich, Ann 4: 637

SIGINT 3: 517, 519

Sikhs 3: 497

Silent Spring 2: 230, 232, 235

Silicone breast implants 2: **351–56,** 352 (ill.)

Simpson, George 1: 84

Singapore International Monetary Exchange 4: 705

Sinn Féin 3: 489, 493

Sirica, John J. 4: 652, 652 (ill.), 657

Sitting Bull 3: 467

$64,000 Question 4: 641, 643

SLAC (Stanford Linear Accelerator Center) 2: 310

Sloan, Hugh 4: 652

Smith, Derrick 4: 701

Smith, E. J. 2: 201

Smith, Jedediah 1: 85

Smith, Margaret Chase 4: 631

Smith, Michael 2: 323, 327

Smoke detectors 2: 307

Snake Brigade 1: 83

Snook, Neta 1: 158

Sobell, Morton 4: 638–39

Society Islands 1: 68

Socrates 3: 375; 4: 573

Soldier's Medal 3: 541

Soucy, Jean-Yves 4: 619

South Island 1: 68

South Pole 1: 144, 146, 147

South Vietnamese 2: 275

Southampton Insurrection 4: **591–94**

Southeast Asia Treaty Organization 3: 543

Space shuttle 2: 320, 323–25, 328

Spanish Armada 3: 393

Spanish Inquisition 4: 577

Sparta 3: 371, 372, 373, 376

Spartan-Halley comet research observatory 2: 323

Speculator Mine Fire 2: 191, 192, 194

Speke, John Hanning 1: 110, 112

Spindler, Karl 3: 490

Spirit of Freedom Memorial 2: 453

Spongiform Encephalopathy Advisory Committee 2: 361, 362

Sprague, Thomas 3: 519

Sprenger, Jacob 4: 575, 576

Spruce Goose 2: **244–52,** 249 (ill.)

Sputnik 4: 641

SSC (Superconducting Super Collider) 2: **309–14**

St. Clair, Arthur 3: 411

St. Elmo's Fire 2: 228

Standard Model 2: 311

Stanley, Henry Morton 1: 109 (ill.), 111, 112, 130

Stans, Maurice 4: 653, 656

Star Wars 4: 660

Stearns, George L. 3: 447

Stempel, Herbert 4: 643, 645, 646, 648

Stephen of Cloyes 1: 7–13; 3: 392

Stevens, Robert T. 4: 631

Stopford, Lieutenant General 3: 472–73

Strong, George C. 3: 449

Stuart, James Ewell Brown 3: 456, 457, 459

Stuckey, Gaylord 1: 168

Suffren 1: 123

Sullivan, Sport 4: 611

Sulpicians 1: 59

Sunchaser 4: 663

Superfund Law 2: 239, 243

Superfund site 2: 193 (ill.), 196

Susi 1: 110, 112, 113

Suvla Bay landing 3: 469, 471, 475

Swigert, John L. 2: 283, 287

Symbion 2: 218

Syracuse 3: 371–72, 374, 375

T

Tahiti 1: 65–67

Taiwanese National Expedition 1: 188, 189

Taske, John 1:183, 1: 184

Taylor, Elizabeth 4: 564

TDRS (Data-Relay Satellite) 2: 323

Technical Services Squad 4: 681

Tecumpease 3: 410

Tecumseh 3: 409–16, 410 (ill.)

Tecumseh's campaign 3: 409–16

Temple, Shirley 4: 617

Tennyson, Alfred 3: 438

Tenskwatawa 3: 412, 421

10th Connecticut Regiment 3: 449

Tenting on the Plains 3: 465

Terra Nova 1: 146, 147

Terry , Alfred H. 3: 465

Tet Offensive 3: 540

Thalidomide 2: 253–58, 257 (ill.)

Thompson, David 1: 89

Thompson, Hugh 3: 541

Thornburgh, Richard 2: 299

Three Mile Island accident 2: 295–301, 296 (ill.)

Throgmorton, Elizabeth 1: 42

Thucydides 3: 374

Tiguex War 1: 37

Timbuktu 1: 77

Tissaphernes 3: 375

Titanic 2: 198–208, 200 (ill.), 202 (ill.), 205 (ill.)

Titanic (film) 4: 666, 667

Tituba 4: 579

To the Top of the Continent 1: 138

Tojo, Hideki 3: 513

Tokyo nerve gas strike 4: 711–16, 714 (ill.)

Tonti, Henry de 1: 60, 61

Tovar, Pedro de 1: 36

Toyoda, Soemu 3: 515–16

Trans Alaska Pipeline 2: 342, 342

Travis, Joseph 4: 592

Treaty of Fort Wayne 3: 414

Treaty of Greenville 3: 411, 412

Trench warfare 3: 476–78, 477 (ill.)

Tresham, Francis 4: 582

The Triangle Shirtwaist Company fire 4: 600–606, 602 (ill.), 603 (ill.), 605 (ill.)

Truman, Harry S 3: 521, 525; 4: 628

Tulloch, Alexander 3: 435, 436

Tullock, Samuel 1: 86

Tupac Amaru Revolutionary Movement 4: 717, 718, 721, 723

Turner, Nat 4: 591–94, 592 (ill.)

Turner, Nathaniel 3: 448

Turturro, John 4: 648

TWA (Trans World Airlines) 2: 244, 260

TWA Super Constellation-DC-10 crash 2: 259–64, 261 (ill.)

TWA Super G Constellation 2: 246

Twenty-One quiz show scandal 4: 641–49

Tydings, Millard 4: 630

Tyne, Frank "Billy" 4: 691–93

U

Udall, Stewart 2: 234

Ulffson, Gunnbjörn 1: 1

Ulrica Leonora 3: 404

Umar 3: 387

UN (United Nations) 3: 521, 523, 525–27

Unabomber 4: 590

Underboss 4: 686

Underground Railroad 4: 594

Union Carbide 2: 315, 319

Union Conscription Act 3: 446

United Airlines DC-7 2:

United Artists 4: 661, 662

United States Department of Commerce 2: 262

United States Department of Defense 2: 276

United States Department of Energy 2: 313

United States Justice Department 4: 671

United States Veterans Administration 2: 278, 281

Universal Pictures 4: 665

University of Toronto 4: 615

Unsafe at Any Speed 2: 265,

Urban II 1: 8

V

Van de Graaf, Robert Jemison 2: 309

Van Doren, Carl 4: 647

Van Doren, Charles 4: 644, 644 (ill.), 645, 647, 648

Van Doren, Geraldine Bernstein 4: 648

Van Doren, Mark 4: 647

Vance, Cyrus 3: 548

Vaught, James 3: 548, 550

Veer, Gerrit de 1: 55

Velásquez, Diego 1: 25, 26

Venus 1: 65

Vertefeuille, Jeanne 4: 679, 680

Viet Cong 2: 273, 275, 277; 3: 536, 537, 539, 542, 543

Vietnam Veterans' Memorial 3: 541, 544, 544 (ill.)

Vietnam War 3: 536–45; 4: 661

Villiers, George 3: 393, 394, 394 (ill.)

Visturs, Ed *1:* 188

Volkswagen *2:* 266

The Voyage of the Discovery *1:* 144, 146

W

Wade, Robert *4:* 680

Walken, Christopher *4:* 661

Walsh, David *4:* 725, 725 (ill.), 727, 728, 729

Walsh, Jeannette *4:* 728

Walsh, Lawrence E. *3:* 551

War of 1812 *3:* 414, 418, 421, 422; *4:* 588

The War of the Worlds (novel) *4:* 621, 623

The War of the Worlds broadcast *4:* **621–25**

Warner Brothers *4:* 663, 664

Washington, George *3:* 405–08, 406 (ill.)

The Washington Post *4:* 651, 653

The Watergate scandal *4:* **650–59**

Waterworld *4:* 660, 665

Wayne, Anthony *3:* 411, 411 (ill.)

We are Five: The Dionne Quintuplets *4:* 619

Weathers, Seaborn Beck *1:* 183, 185, 186 (ill.), 187, 188

Weaver, George "Buck" *4:* 608, 609, 613

Webb, Wellington *4:* 671

Weininger, Janet Ray *3:* 533

Welles, Orson *4:* 621, 622 (ill.), 623–25

Wellesley, Arthur Duke of Wellington *3:* 428–29, 431

Wells, H. G. *4:* 621, 623

Westerberg, Wayne *1:* 167, 172

Westmoreland, William C. *3:* 539

Wetterhahn, Karen *2:* **365–70,** 367 (ill.), 369 (ill.)

Whalen, Robert P. *2:* 238

Whiddon, Jacob *1:* 43

White Star Line *2:* 199, 202, 204

White, John *1:* 42, 47

Whitney, Harry *1:* 140, 141

Wicca *4:* 576

Wilentz, Robert *4:* 664

Williams, Claude "Lefty" *4:* 608, 609, 611

Willis, Bruce *4:* 664

Wills, William John *1:* **114–21,** 120 (ill.)

Wilson, Edward *1:* 149

Wilson, Joseph T. *3:* 451

Wilton, Helen *1:* 183, 187

Winfrey, Oprah *2:* 362

Wingina *1:* 49

Winter, Thomas *4:* 581

Winter Olympic Games *4:* 698

Witchcraft hysteria *4:* **575–79**

Witchcraft trial *4:* 578 (ill.)

Witch-hunts *4:* 575, 578, 579

Witness to the Mob *4:* 686

Wolfe, Tom *4:* 663

Wolff, Mary *2:* 236

Women's Air Derby *1:* 160

Woods, Rose Mary *4:* 655

Woodward, Bob *4:* 651–53

World Series *4:* 607, 613

World War I *3:* 470

Wrangel Island *1:* 132

Wright, John *4:* 581

Wright, William *1:* 115, 118, 120

Y

Yakovlev, Anatoli *4:* 635–36

Yamato *3:* 517, 519

Year 2000 computer problem *2:* **345–50**

Young Communist League *4:* 635

Yu-Nan, Chen *1:* 189

Z

Zacatecas *1:* 32

Zapotecs *1:* 28

Zeidler, Othmar *2:* 231

Zelix *1:* 101

Zeppelin Company *2:* 221, 223

Ziegler, Ron *4:* 650